MathFlare

Name: ______________________

Class: __________

Teacher: ______________________

Introduction

As parents and educators, we recognize the pivotal role mathematics plays in shaping a child's academic journey and future success. Yet, the path to mathematical proficiency can often seem daunting, fraught with challenges and complexities. That's where the transformative power of MathFlare Workbooks shine through, illuminating the way forward with clarity, precision, and purpose.

Introducing MathFlare Workbooks – a beacon of guidance, a testament to excellence, and a catalyst for achievement. Crafted with meticulous care and expertise, MathFlare Workbooks stand as paragons of educational excellence, designed to nurture young minds, ignite a passion for learning, and develop a deep-rooted understanding of mathematical concepts.

Picture this: your child eagerly delves into the pages of Mathflare Workbook, greeted by a step-by-step guide illuminated with vivid examples that demystify complex mathematical concepts. With each turn of the page, they embark on a journey of discovery, encountering thoughtfully curated practice questions that reinforce learning and hone problem-solving skills. And when they unveil the answers to those very questions, a sense of accomplishment blossoms within them – a tangible reward for their hard work and dedication.

But MathFlare Workbooks are more than just tools for learning; they are pathways to comprehension, fostering a deep-seated understanding of mathematical concepts through a sequential, logical flow. From fundamental principles to advanced problem-solving strategies, every chapter builds upon the last, ensuring a robust foundation upon which future knowledge can be constructed.

As parents, we yearn for nothing more than to see our children thrive, to witness the spark of inspiration ignited within them as they conquer academic challenges with confidence and poise. MathFlare Workbooks serve as partners in this noble endeavor, offering not just practice questions, but the keys to unlocking a world of opportunity.

And for teachers, MathFlare Workbooks stand as invaluable allies in the quest to cultivate mathematical proficiency in the classroom. With answers readily available, instructors can focus on guiding and nurturing their students, confident in the knowledge that MathFlare Workbooks provide a solid framework upon which to build.

In the pages of MathFlare Workbooks, we find not just the promise of academic excellence, but the seeds of a brighter tomorrow. So let us embrace the power of mathematics, let us champion the journey of learning, and let us pave the way for a generation of young minds poised to shape the world. With MathFlare Workbooks as our guide, the possibilities are infinite, and the future, bright.

Table of Contents

Chapter. 01
Addition and Subtraction

Addition with Regrouping	1
Subtraction with Regrouping	5
Adding Decimals	11
Subtracting Decimals	14
Addition (3 Addend)	17

Chapter. 02
Multiplication and Division

Multiplication: (Double Digit)	20
Multiplication: (3 Digit)	23
Multiplying Decimals	26
Dividing Decimals	33
Long Division with Remainders	40
Using the Power of 10	47
Multiplication Word Problems	52
Division Word Problems	60

Chapter. 03
Factors and Multiples

Factors	70
Multiples	75

Chapter. 04
Place Value and Expanded Notations

Place Value	80
Place Value and Expanded Notations	85

Chapter. 05
Fractions

Equivalent Fractions	106
Fractions Addition (Common Denominator)	109
Fractions Subtraction (Common Denominator)	115

Fractions Multiplication	121
Fractions Division	124

Chapter. 06
Geometry

Area and Perimeter	127

Chapter. 07 — 140
Roman Numerals

Chapter. 08
Unit Conversion

Metric Weights and Measures	145
Metric Conversion	148

Answers

MathFlare
MATH WORKBOOK
Grade 2
Step by Step Guide and Essential Practice with Answers
Addition Subtraction
Multiplication
Place Value and Expanded Notations
Geometry
MathFlare Publishing

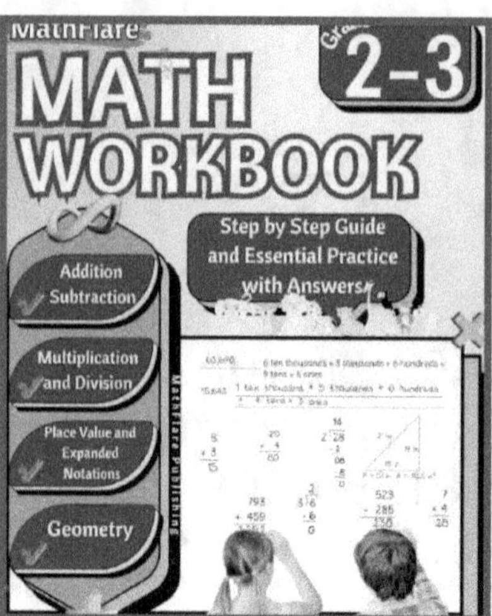
MathFlare
MATH WORKBOOK
Grade 2-3
Step by Step Guide and Essential Practice with Answers
Addition Subtraction
Multiplication and Division
Place Value and Expanded Notations
Geometry
MathFlare Publishing

MathFlare
MATH WORKBOOK
Grade 3
Step by Step Guide and Essential Practice with Answers
Multiplication and Division
Decimals
Place Value and Expanded Notations
Fractions and Geometry
MathFlare Publishing

MathFlare
MATH WORKBOOK
Grade 1
Step by Step Guide and Essential Practice with Answers
Counting and Numbers
Addition and Subtraction
Place Value and Expanded Notations
Understanding Time
MathFlare Publishing

MathFlare
MATH WORKBOOK
Grade 1-2
Step by Step Guide and Essential Practice with Answers
Counting and Numbers
Addition and Subtraction
Place Value and Expanded Notations
Understanding Time
MathFlare Publishing

MathFlare
MATH WORKBOOK
Grade 3-4
Step by Step Guide and Essential Practice with Answers
Addition Subtraction
Multiplication Division
Place Value and Expanded Notations
Fractions and Geometry
MathFlare Publishing

MathFlare
MATH WORKBOOK
Grade 4
Step by Step Guide and Essential Practice with Answers
Addition Subtraction
Multiplication Division
Place Value and Expanded Notations
Fractions and Geometry
MathFlare Publishing

MathFlare
MATH WORKBOOK
Grade 4-5
Step by Step Guide and Essential Practice with Answers
Multiplication Division
Place Value and Expanded Notations
Fractions and Geometry
Unit Conversion
MathFlare Publishing

MathFlare
Grade 5
MATH
WORKBOOK
Step by Step Guide
and Essential Practice
with Answers
Multiplication
Division
Place Value and
Expanded
Notations
Fractions
and Geometry
Unit
Conversion
MathFlare Publishing

MathFlare
Grade 5-6
MATH
WORKBOOK
Step by Step Guide
and Essential Practice
with Answers
Multiplication
Division
Place Value and
Expanded
Notations
Fractions
and Geometry
Units and
Statistics
MathFlare Publishing

MathFlare
Grade 6
MATH
WORKBOOK
Step by Step Guide
and Essential Practice
with Answers
Integers and
Statistics
Arithmetic and
Pre-Algebra
Fractions
and Geometry
Ratio and
Percentage
MathFlare Publishing

MathFlare
Grade 6-7
MATH
WORKBOOK
Step by Step Guide
and Essential Practice
with Answers
Arithmetic and
Pre-Algebra
Ratio, Percent
Proportion
Geometry
Statistics
MathFlare Publishing

MathFlare
Grade 7
MATH
WORKBOOK
Step by Step Guide
and Essential Practice
with Answers
Pre-Algebra
Ratio, Percent
Proportion
Geometry
Statistics
MathFlare Publishing

MathFlare
Grade 7-8
MATH
WORKBOOK
Step by Step Guide
and Essential Practice
with Answers
Pre-Algebra
Ratio, Percent
Proportion
Geometry and
Cartesian
Plane
Statistics
MathFlare Publishing

MathFlare
Grade 8-9
MATH
WORKBOOK
Step by Step Guide
and Essential Practice
with Answers
Pre-Algebra
Ratio, Proportion
and Percentage
Linear
Equations
Geometry and
Cartesian Plane
MathFlare Publishing

MathFlare
Grade 8
MATH
WORKBOOK
Step by Step Guide
and Essential Practice
with Answers
Pre-Algebra
Percentage
Linear
Equations
Geometry
MathFlare Publishing

Chapter. 01

Addition and Subtraction

Addition with Regrouping

When we do addition, we combine numbers. But sometimes, when we're adding numbers, we might need to regroup. Regrouping means we have to move a number from one place to another, usually to the next column, to get the right answer.

For Example: Let's take an example of adding 6533 and 7579 together:

$$5\ 6\ 5\ 3\ 3$$
$$+6\ 7\ 5\ 7\ 9$$

First, we start by adding the digits in the ones place: 3 + 9 = 12. We write down the 2 in the ones place and carry over the 1 to the tens place.

$$1$$
$$5\ 6\ 5\ 3\ 3$$
$$+6\ 7\ 5\ 7\ 9$$
$$2$$

Now, we add the digits in the tens place, along with the carry-over: 3 + 7 + 1 = 11. We write down the 1 in the tens place and carry over the 1 to the hundreds place.

$$1\ 1$$
$$5\ 6\ 5\ 3\ 3$$
$$+6\ 7\ 5\ 7\ 9$$
$$1\ 2$$

Now, we add the digits in the hundreds place, along with the carry-over: 5 + 5 + 1 = 11. We write down the 1 in the tens place and carry over the 1 to the hundreds place.

$$
\begin{array}{r}
1\ 1\ \ \ \ \\
5\ 6\ 5\ 3\ 3 \\
+6\ 7\ 5\ 7\ 9 \\
\hline
1\ 1\ 2
\end{array}
$$

Now, we add the digits in the thousandth place, along with the carry-over: 6 + 7 + 1 = 14.

$$
\begin{array}{r}
1\ 1\ 1\ \ \ \ \\
5\ 6\ 5\ 3\ 3 \\
+6\ 7\ 5\ 7\ 9 \\
\hline
4\ 1\ 1\ 2
\end{array}
$$

Now, we add the digits in the ten-thousandth place, along with the carry-over: 5 + 6 + 1 = 12.

$$
\begin{array}{r}
1\ 1\ 1\ 1\ \ \ \ \\
5\ 6\ 5\ 3\ 3 \\
+6\ 7\ 5\ 7\ 9 \\
\hline
1\ 2\ 4\ 1\ 1\ 2
\end{array}
$$

This process of carrying over helps us accurately add numbers, especially when they're larger.

Subtraction with Regrouping

Subtraction is a key math operation where we find the difference between two numbers. Sometimes, when we subtract, we might need to regroup, which means borrowing from the next column.

MathFlare - Math Workbook 4th Grade

Let's take an example of subtracting 8436 from 6563:

First, we start by subtracting the digits in the ones place: 3 - 6.

Since 3 is less than 6, we need to regroup. We borrow 1 from the tens place, making it 5 tens instead of 6, and add it to the ones place.

So, 3 becomes 13, and then we subtract 6.

$$
\begin{array}{r}
8\ 5\ 6\ 13 \\
-6\ 4\ 3\ 6 \\
\hline
7
\end{array}
$$

Now, we subtract the tens place digits: 5 - 3 = 2

$$
\begin{array}{r}
5 \\
8\ 5\ \cancel{6}\ 13 \\
-6\ 4\ 3\ 6 \\
\hline
2\ 7
\end{array}
$$

Now, we subtract the hundreds place digits: 5 - 4 = 1

$$
\begin{array}{r}
5 \\
8\ 5\ \cancel{6}\ 13 \\
-6\ 4\ 3\ 6 \\
\hline
1\ 2\ 7
\end{array}
$$

Now, we subtract the hundreds place digits: 8 - 6 = 2

$$
\begin{array}{r}
5 \\
8\ 5\ \cancel{6}\ 13 \\
-6\ 4\ 3\ 6 \\
\hline
2\ 1\ 2\ 7
\end{array}
$$

This process of regrouping or borrowing helps us accurately subtract numbers, especially when the top digit is smaller than the bottom one.

Let's solve problems from exercises:

$$\begin{array}{r} {}^{1\ 1\ 1\ 1}59{,}574 \\ +\ \ \ 6{,}576 \\ \hline 66{,}150 \end{array} \qquad \begin{array}{r} 97{,}120 \\ -\ \ \ 7{,}383 \\ \hline 89{,}737 \end{array}$$

Adding Decimals

Adding decimals is like adding whole numbers, but we must align the decimal points carefully. For instance, when adding 49.88 and 45.78:

Step 1: Align the decimal points.

$$\begin{array}{r} 49.88 \\ +\ 45.78 \end{array}$$

Step 2: Start adding from the rightmost digit (the ones place) and move to the left.
Add 8 and 8: 8 + 8 = 16. Write down 6 in the ones place and carry over 1 to the tenths place.

$$\begin{array}{r} 49.88 \\ +\ 45.78 \\ \hline 6 \end{array}$$

Step 3: Add the tenths place.
Add 1 (carried over from the previous step), 8, and 7: 1 + 8 + 7 = 16. Write down 6 in the tenths place and carry over 1 to the hundredths place.

$$\begin{array}{r} 49.88 \\ +\ 45.78 \\ \hline 66 \end{array}$$

<u>Step 4: Continue adding digits to the left until you reach the leftmost digit:</u>

$$49.88$$
$$+\ 45.78$$
$$9566$$

<u>Step 5: Finally, write the sum with the decimal point directly below the decimal points in the original numbers.</u>

$$49.88$$
$$+\ 45.78$$
$$95.66$$

Subtracting Decimals

Subtracting decimals follows a process like adding decimals, except instead of adding the numbers, we subtract them.

Let's solve more problems:

$$176.07$$
$$+\ 765.69$$
$$941.76$$

$$738.71$$
$$-\ 715.74$$
$$22.97$$

Addition (3 Addends)

To add three numbers (3 addends) together, we simply add them one by one.

Let's solve a problem.

$$1\ 1\ 1$$
$$6{,}533$$
$$4{,}727$$
$$+\ 6{,}102$$
$$17{,}362$$

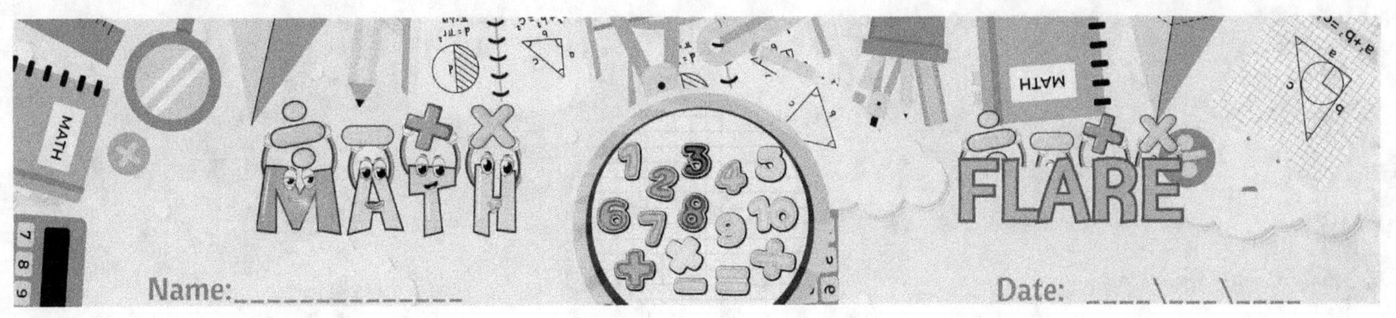

Addition with Regrouping

Find the sum.

1)
```
 1 1  1 1
  59,574
+  6,576
---------
  66,150
```

2)
```
  49,179
+  8,998
---------
```

3)
```
  59,518
+  5,894
---------
```

4)
```
  38,334
+  6,976
---------
```

5)
```
  71,379
+  9,869
---------
```

6)
```
  55,437
+  6,673
---------
```

7)
```
  91,589
+  9,827
---------
```

8)
```
  31,131
+  9,999
---------
```

9)
```
  59,495
+  6,848
---------
```

10)
```
  19,212
+  5,899
---------
```

11)
```
  66,417
+  4,697
---------
```

12)
```
  74,677
+  7,756
---------
```

13)
```
  72,626
+  9,498
---------
```

14)
```
  37,161
+  4,969
---------
```

15)
```
  39,314
+  8,898
---------
```

16)
```
  82,217
+  8,896
---------
```

17)
```
  35,575
+  9,638
---------
```

18)
```
  29,998
+  8,767
---------
```

19)
```
  71,452
+  9,868
---------
```

20)
```
  86,425
+  7,897
---------
```

21) 75,479 + 8,943	22) 52,961 + 9,299	23) 69,168 + 9,958	24) 92,111 + 9,999
25) 61,628 + 9,497	26) 17,515 + 4,597	27) 88,275 + 2,845	28) 64,895 + 9,579
29) 91,562 + 9,698	30) 18,357 + 4,954	31) 23,283 + 9,928	32) 41,416 + 9,995
33) 26,483 + 5,767	34) 41,465 + 9,886	35) 28,172 + 4,948	36) 72,784 + 8,428
37) 81,991 + 9,729	38) 82,841 + 9,699	39) 91,911 + 9,299	40) 18,135 + 7,985

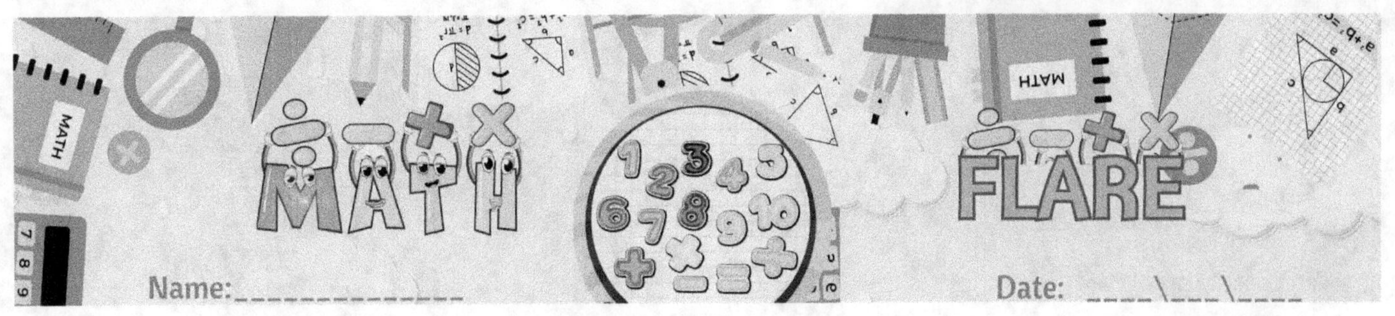

41)	32,878 + 9,962	42)	85,514 + 6,997	43)	77,611 + 5,499	44)	24,486 + 6,788
45)	57,429 + 8,689	46)	97,157 + 9,967	47)	69,896 + 5,388	48)	58,695 + 8,528
49)	59,122 + 6,999	50)	95,847 + 7,679	51)	64,124 + 8,987	52)	19,356 + 2,868
53)	51,884 + 9,627	54)	59,221 + 5,889	55)	35,556 + 8,794	56)	34,792 + 8,828
57)	63,941 + 8,169	58)	21,661 + 9,969	59)	16,675 + 8,577	60)	17,661 + 7,549

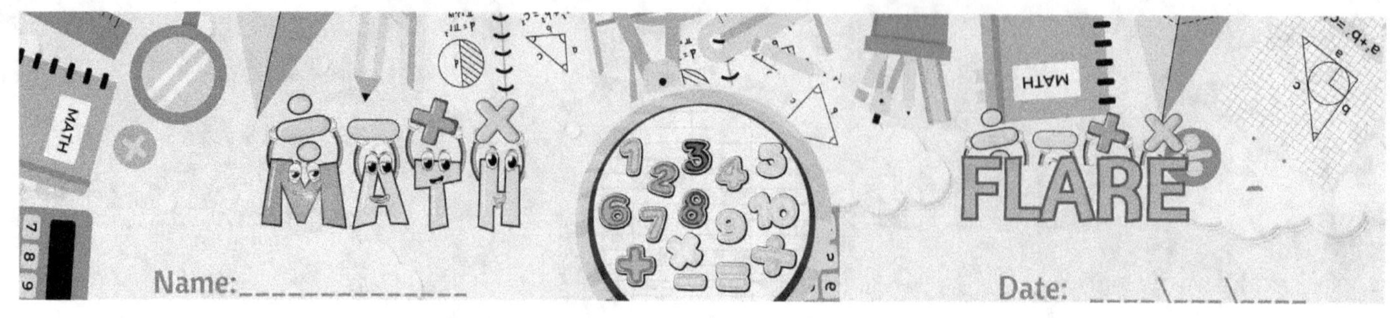

61) 38,189 + 2,929	62) 31,836 + 9,388	63) 45,351 + 7,989	64) 21,344 + 9,888
65) 88,526 + 9,994	66) 27,947 + 3,369	67) 66,498 + 9,763	68) 23,913 + 9,997
69) 91,276 + 9,979	70) 72,761 + 9,989	71) 91,784 + 9,348	72) 91,621 + 9,999
73) 79,513 + 6,898	74) 45,537 + 9,997	75) 41,225 + 9,888	76) 76,614 + 4,596
77) 61,138 + 9,977	78) 88,213 + 5,898	79) 92,998 + 9,547	80) 82,867 + 8,857

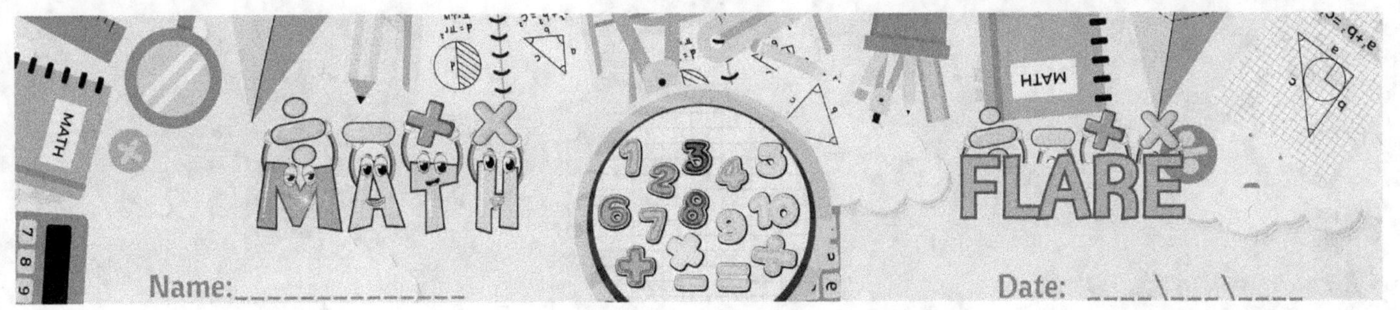

81) 24,931 + 7,979	82) 62,525 + 8,689	83) 69,978 + 1,158	84) 71,718 + 9,599
85) 26,417 + 5,995	86) 33,373 + 7,938	87) 53,119 + 9,993	88) 83,693 + 7,477
89) 31,666 + 9,679	90) 44,373 + 7,857	91) 37,771 + 8,579	92) 99,881 + 5,349
93) 32,937 + 8,489	94) 73,173 + 7,959	95) 13,438 + 7,997	96) 26,144 + 9,979
97) 84,426 + 9,998	98) 36,397 + 7,766	99) 21,917 + 9,596	100) 99,524 + 7,796

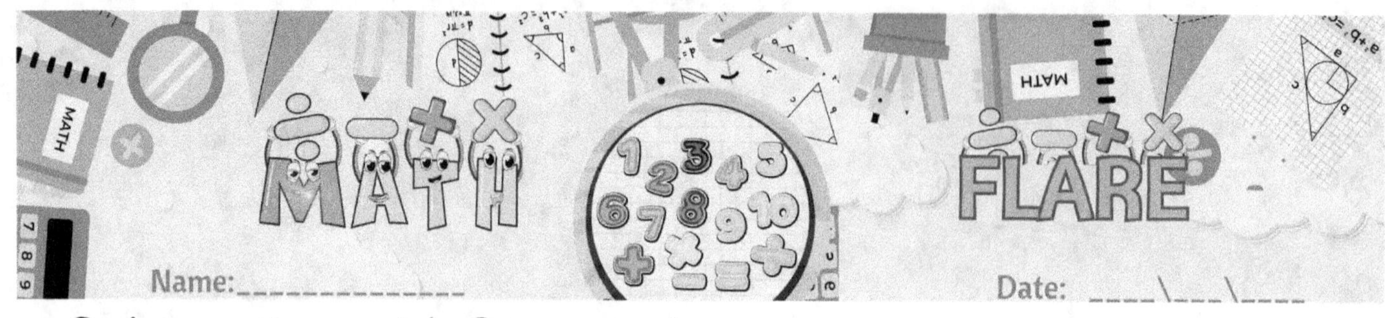

Subtraction with Regrouping

Find the difference.

1) 97,120 − 7,383 89,737	2) 23,170 − 3,787	3) 21,670 − 3,793	4) 90,240 − 9,371
5) 46,670 − 3,884	6) 29,170 − 4,486	7) 61,100 − 1,636	8) 50,800 − 4,916
9) 29,230 − 1,964	10) 13,060 − 8,597	11) 38,400 − 3,559	12) 68,850 − 5,983
13) 86,570 − 3,887	14) 64,850 − 5,982	15) 39,830 − 2,992	16) 53,840 − 6,994
17) 61,800 − 6,944	18) 79,380 − 6,493	19) 68,580 − 7,797	20) 41,800 − 9,969

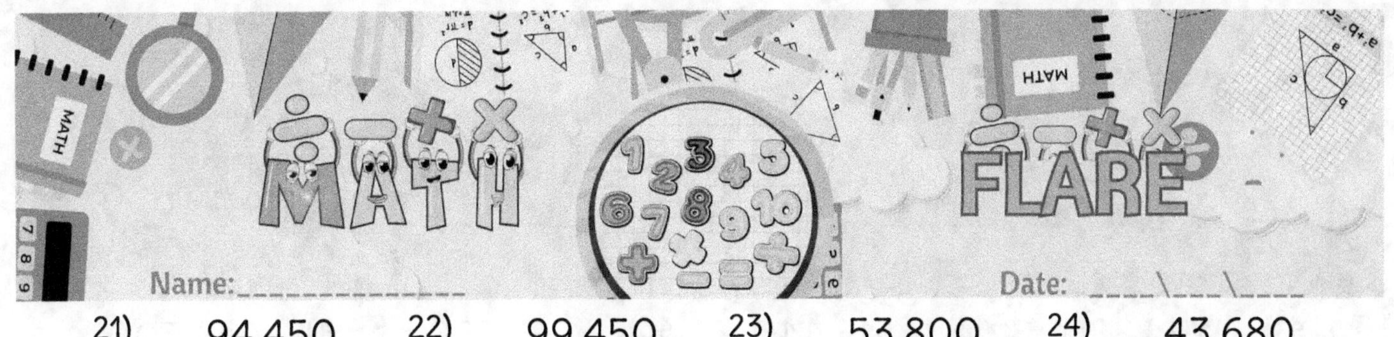

21) 94,450 − 7,976	22) 99,450 − 7,998	23) 53,800 − 8,937	24) 43,680 − 7,896
25) 53,370 − 9,583	26) 53,430 − 1,786	27) 62,540 − 2,664	28) 49,510 − 7,652
29) 14,370 − 6,983	30) 51,030 − 8,359	31) 72,280 − 4,491	32) 63,770 − 3,885
33) 79,580 − 6,692	34) 79,860 − 9,985	35) 36,860 − 8,986	36) 74,560 − 5,696
37) 77,230 − 1,746	38) 90,820 − 5,993	39) 36,130 − 8,886	40) 99,420 − 1,745

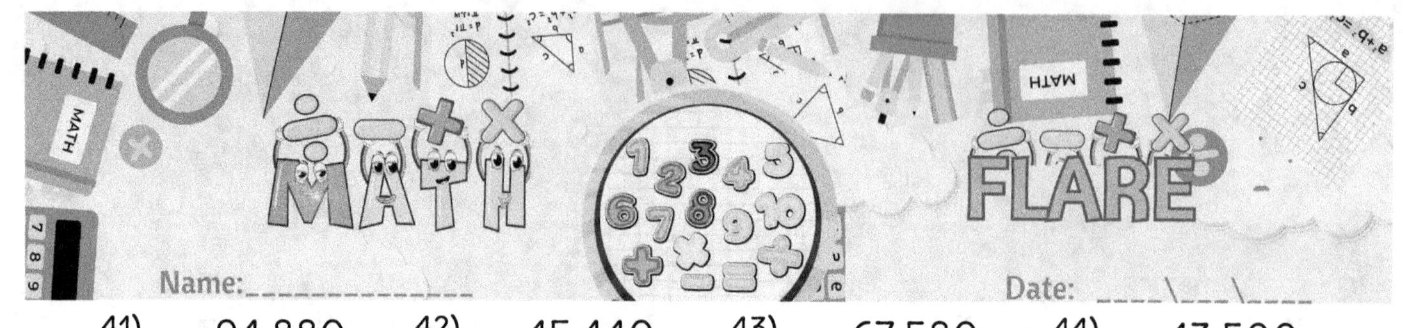

41)	94,880 - 8,997	42)	15,440 - 4,678	43)	67,580 - 5,798	44)	13,500 - 4,756
45)	26,830 - 1,986	46)	60,150 - 9,875	47)	31,240 - 5,871	48)	33,420 - 6,773
49)	25,680 - 7,999	50)	10,380 - 9,497	51)	14,510 - 4,983	52)	51,100 - 6,712
53)	28,660 - 9,876	54)	34,620 - 5,938	55)	33,410 - 9,757	56)	45,380 - 2,591
57)	70,410 - 4,883	58)	88,210 - 8,539	59)	35,870 - 2,987	60)	68,060 - 3,781

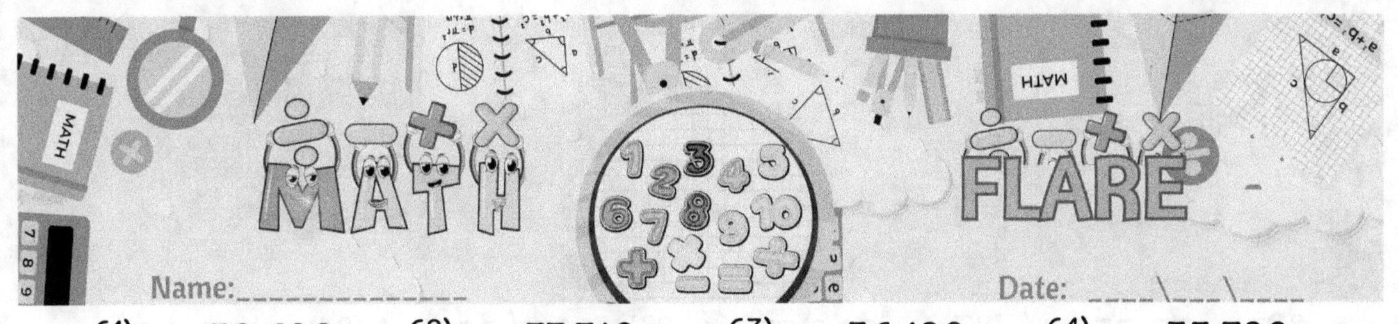

61) 59,620 − 4,989	62) 77,710 − 2,981	63) 36,120 − 7,586	64) 35,720 − 2,852
65) 83,840 − 3,979	66) 43,240 − 6,774	67) 88,470 − 1,884	68) 97,670 − 5,784
69) 45,780 − 4,894	70) 28,030 − 7,161	71) 27,360 − 5,881	72) 24,150 − 3,666
73) 72,460 − 4,794	74) 38,340 − 8,667	75) 70,480 − 4,892	76) 37,060 − 9,872
77) 15,730 − 7,978	78) 41,160 − 7,281	79) 71,310 − 3,499	80) 40,880 − 5,996

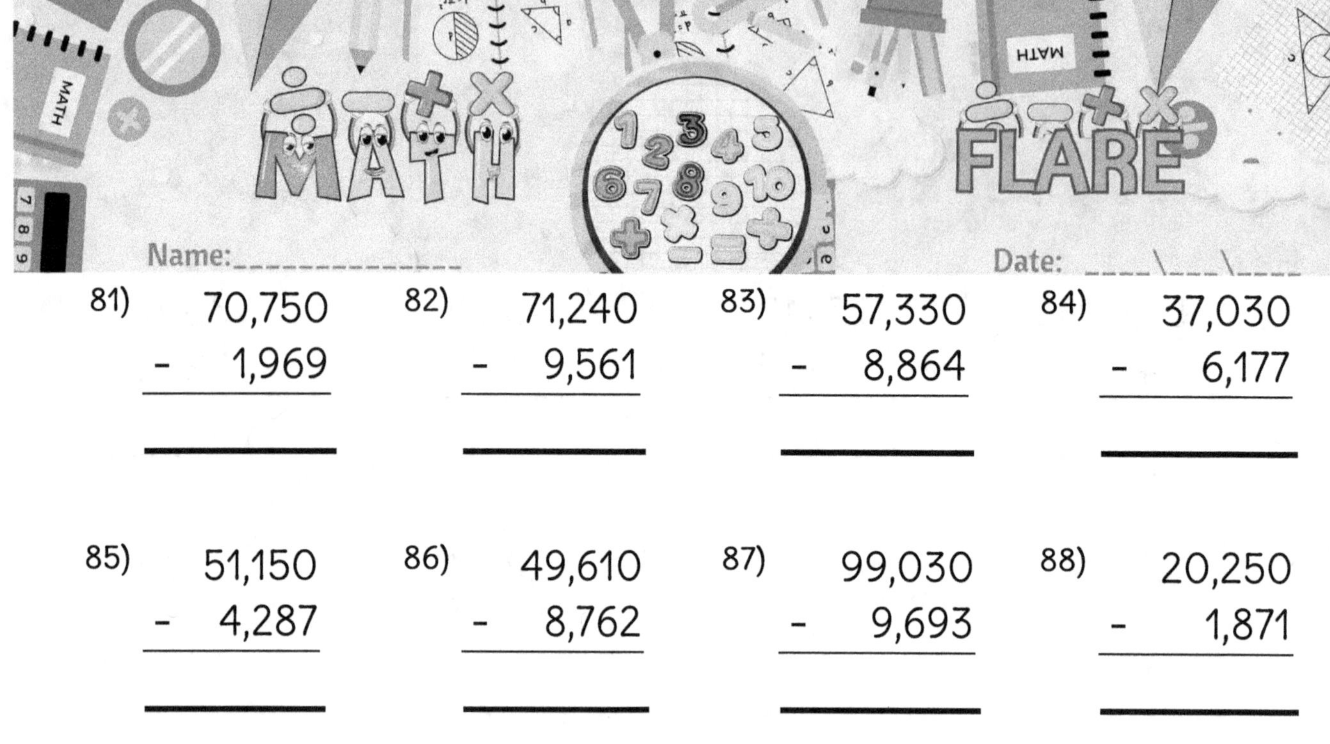

81)   70,750
  − 1,969
	82) 71,240
	  − 9,561
		83) 57,330
		  − 8,864
			84) 37,030
			  − 6,177

85)   51,150
  − 4,287
	86) 49,610
	  − 8,762
		87) 99,030
		  − 9,693
			88) 20,250
			  − 1,871

89)   28,140
  − 5,386
	90) 56,640
	  − 9,887
		91) 47,460
		  − 5,991
			92) 58,030
			  − 4,592

93)   10,720
  − 4,861
	94) 56,600
	  − 2,869
		95) 77,470
		  − 3,586
			96) 84,520
			  − 2,779

97)   17,350
  − 7,586
	98) 10,360
	  − 2,986
		99) 87,070
		  − 2,893
			100) 79,020
			  − 8,941

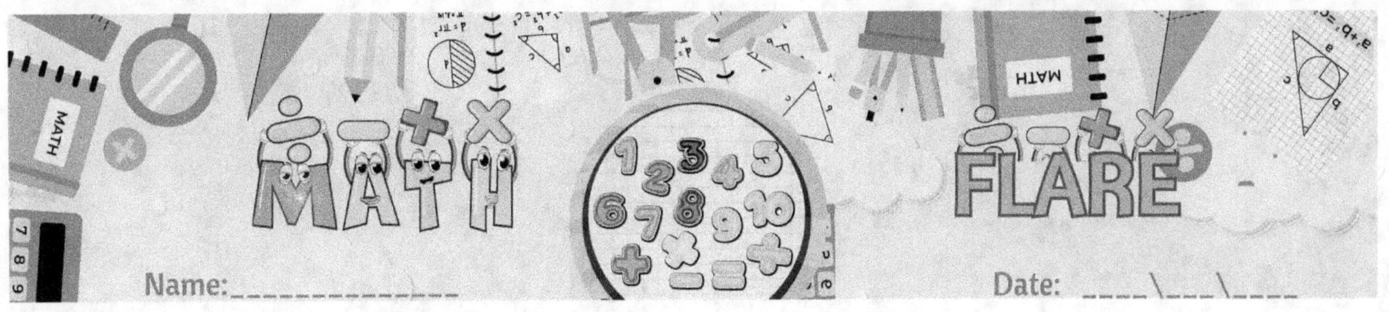

Adding Decimals

Find the sum.

1)   176.07
  + 765.69
  ——————
     941.76

2)   412.46
  + 381.20
  ——————

3)   984.04
  + 494.32
  ——————

4)   995.86
  + 187.92
  ——————

5)   625.32
  + 398.57
  ——————

6)   540.77
  + 299.57
  ——————

7)   753.43
  + 495.08
  ——————

8)   153.97
  + 274.32
  ——————

9)   580.71
  + 353.18
  ——————

10) 948.88
  + 227.18
  ——————

11) 364.45
  + 213.45
  ——————

12) 842.94
  + 256.97
  ——————

13) 578.49
  + 358.23
  ——————

14) 802.77
  + 338.71
  ——————

15) 965.77
  + 989.92
  ——————

16) 242.29
  + 996.08
  ——————

17) 723.37
  + 672.29
  ——————

18) 838.70
  + 708.94
  ——————

19) 220.72
  + 299.10
  ——————

20) 475.17
  + 612.96
  ——————

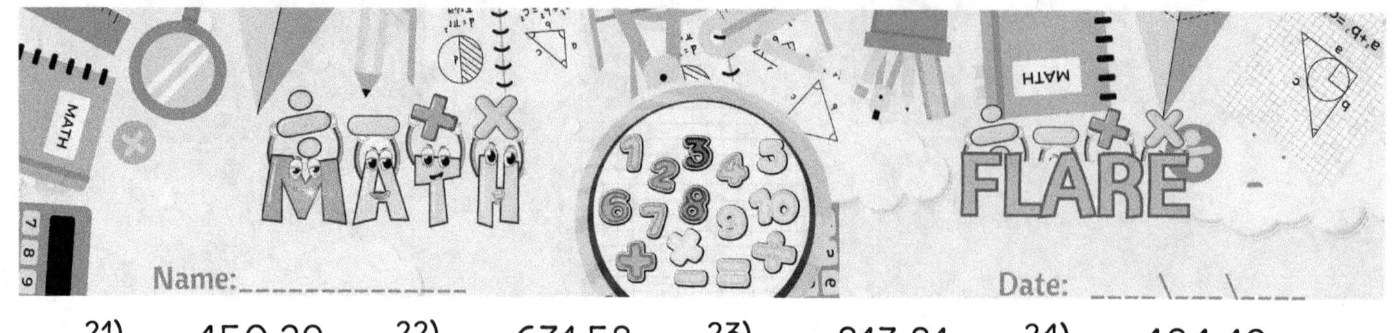

21)	450.29 + 478.12	22)	631.58 + 476.20	23)	813.81 + 645.66	24)	484.49 + 678.45
25)	697.70 + 829.33	26)	631.86 + 617.57	27)	336.44 + 663.05	28)	629.70 + 962.61
29)	922.74 + 255.50	30)	802.70 + 725.80	31)	691.54 + 757.15	32)	222.14 + 635.39
33)	256.28 + 544.68	34)	576.19 + 181.13	35)	656.37 + 445.02	36)	153.61 + 381.60
37)	878.00 + 435.92	38)	776.89 + 886.32	39)	581.86 + 466.73	40)	443.15 + 932.82

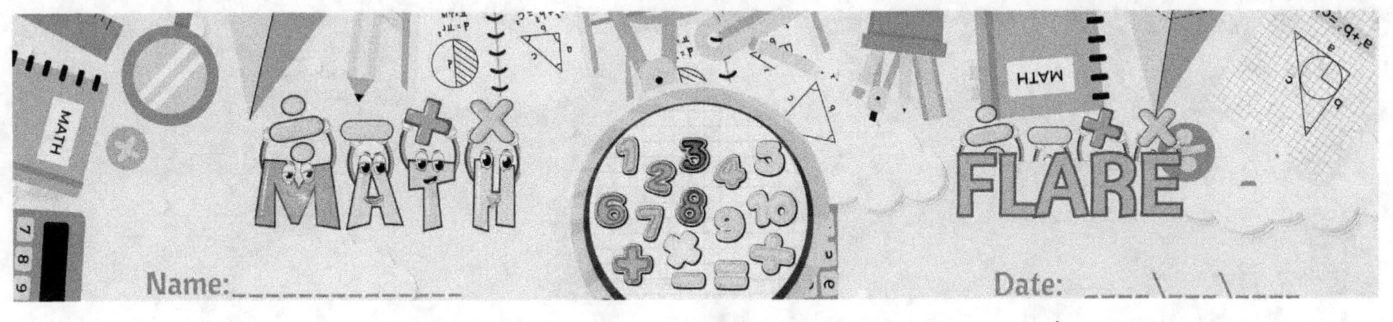

41)   873.73
    + 224.32
    ____

42)   641.00
    + 236.44
    ____

43)   458.06
    + 624.71
    ____

44)   759.64
    + 160.32
    ____

45)   142.59
    + 876.08
    ____

46)   786.19
    + 965.21
    ____

47)   496.39
    + 749.36
    ____

48)   921.41
    + 693.13
    ____

49)   355.99
    + 996.18
    ____

50)   319.92
    + 369.13
    ____

51)   169.48
    + 403.36
    ____

52)   122.08
    + 352.68
    ____

53)   775.73
    + 350.26
    ____

54)   739.56
    + 900.51
    ____

55)   886.15
    + 743.37
    ____

56)   480.75
    + 556.01
    ____

57)   812.34
    + 869.87
    ____

58)   852.06
    + 567.23
    ____

59)   216.15
    + 985.69
    ____

60)   277.33
    + 631.56
    ____

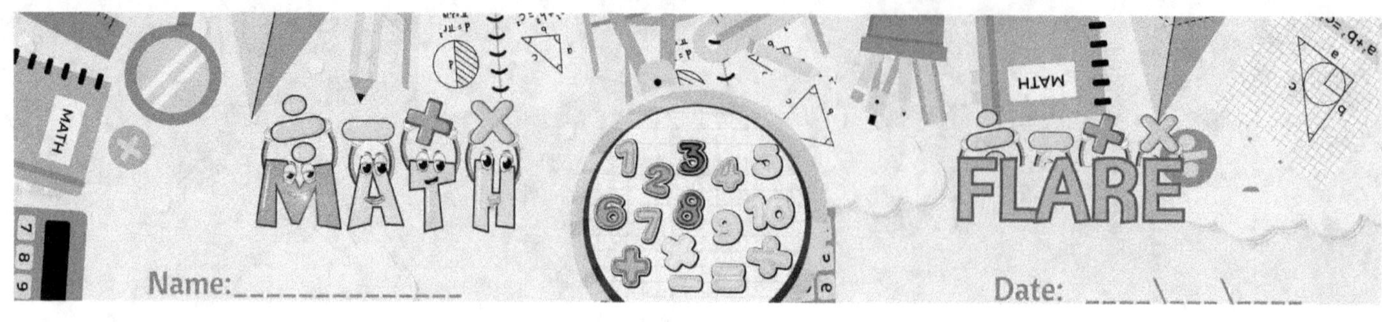

Subtracting Decimals

Find the difference.

1)   738.71
− 715.74

2)   614.76
− 117.47

3)   897.82
− 680.04

4)   903.58
− 429.26

5)   994.62
− 147.40

6)   471.99
− 170.25

7)   539.45
− 484.63

8)   857.54
− 330.87

9)   338.22
− 210.79

10)   334.21
− 316.67

11)   898.97
− 496.09

12)   830.13
− 790.35

13)   693.80
− 219.97

14)   694.88
− 146.81

15)   826.34
− 455.86

16)   836.03
− 149.46

17)   924.19
− 143.35

18)   859.47
− 520.13

19)   515.90
− 287.40

20)   332.39
− 139.49

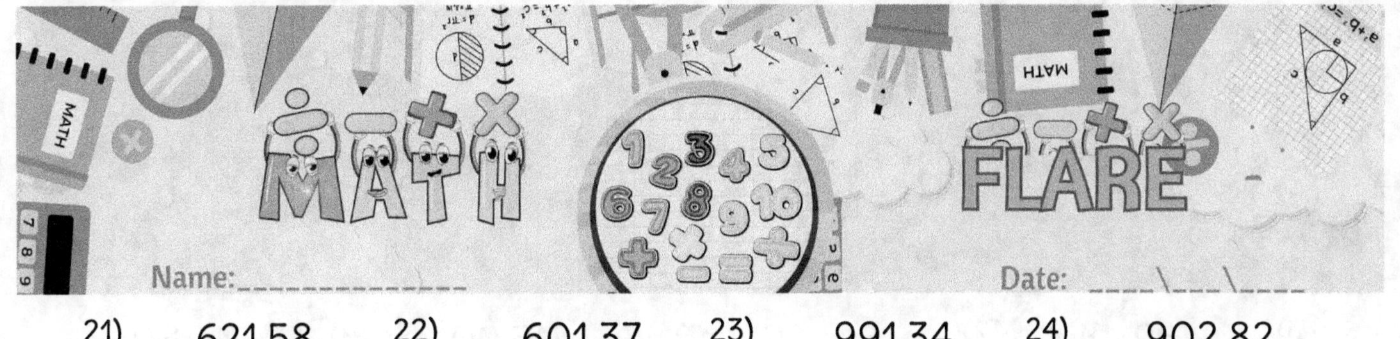

21) 621.58
  − 146.79
  ____

22) 601.37
  − 205.36
  ____

23) 991.34
  − 232.94
  ____

24) 902.82
  − 530.20
  ____

25) 657.63
  − 162.67
  ____

26) 954.66
  − 226.37
  ____

27) 871.94
  − 151.58
  ____

28) 943.24
  − 224.72
  ____

29) 742.04
  − 577.86
  ____

30) 845.29
  − 648.63
  ____

31) 659.13
  − 481.08
  ____

32) 579.27
  − 124.00
  ____

33) 927.36
  − 807.98
  ____

34) 560.74
  − 354.60
  ____

35) 765.27
  − 665.90
  ____

36) 959.45
  − 453.24
  ____

37) 935.39
  − 333.07
  ____

38) 977.97
  − 188.72
  ____

39) 950.92
  − 633.62
  ____

40) 727.95
  − 163.96
  ____

41) 459.44 − 176.14	42) 618.40 − 492.05	43) 415.90 − 395.19	44) 716.50 − 398.46
45) 699.09 − 205.73	46) 941.80 − 499.52	47) 878.91 − 480.22	48) 714.97 − 425.83
49) 605.11 − 133.65	50) 748.96 − 514.90	51) 228.43 − 137.45	52) 928.72 − 814.13
53) 636.83 − 251.03	54) 164.58 − 156.10	55) 967.50 − 739.45	56) 736.27 − 347.73
57) 562.15 − 266.80	58) 319.44 − 305.46	59) 461.17 − 292.58	60) 270.22 − 225.47

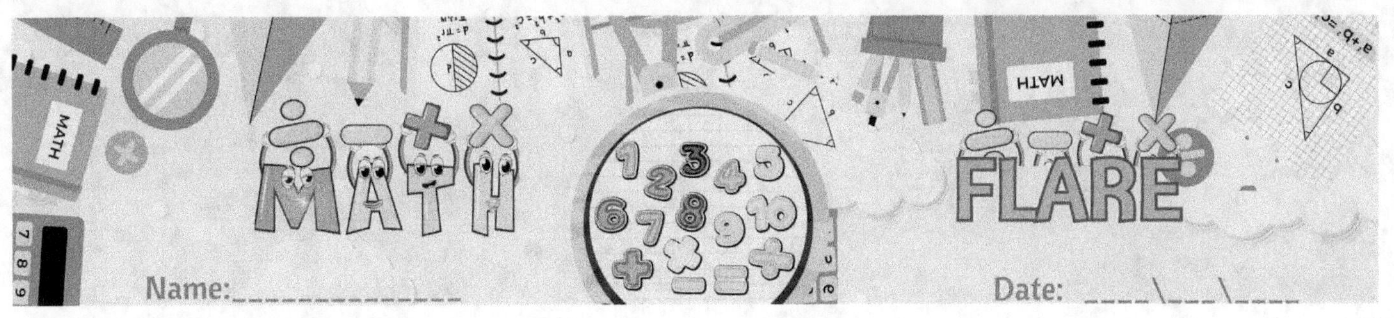

Addition (3 Addends)

Find the sum.

1)
```
  1 1 1
   6,533
   4,727
+  6,102
  ______
  17,362
```

2)
```
   1,635
   6,381
+  3,264
  ______
```

3)
```
   8,705
   7,212
+  7,675
  ______
```

4)
```
   7,523
   5,982
+  4,143
  ______
```

5)
```
   4,257
   2,410
+  7,892
  ______
```

6)
```
   4,126
   1,585
+  8,875
  ______
```

7)
```
   8,804
   1,770
+  7,770
  ______
```

8)
```
   1,965
   5,492
+  9,012
  ______
```

9)
```
   8,369
   8,277
+  3,150
  ______
```

10)
```
   2,890
   7,986
+  5,743
  ______
```

11)
```
   1,595
   5,802
+  1,869
  ______
```

12)
```
   9,907
   8,620
+  7,511
  ______
```

13)
```
   5,010
   8,034
+  7,394
  ______
```

14)
```
   7,084
   2,167
+  3,865
  ______
```

15)
```
   5,285
   7,451
+  1,817
  ______
```

16)
```
   3,636
   6,069
+  2,188
  ______
```

17) 8,869 8,039 + 4,842	18) 8,420 2,004 + 6,330	19) 3,757 5,568 + 9,235	20) 7,090 3,265 + 8,103
21) 1,114 6,815 + 9,225	22) 2,932 6,928 + 1,181	23) 3,275 4,349 + 3,789	24) 1,382 9,115 + 3,551
25) 2,481 2,719 + 9,602	26) 4,905 6,679 + 8,040	27) 8,195 5,734 + 3,208	28) 1,962 4,021 + 9,947
29) 1,900 3,175 + 4,797	30) 5,537 7,150 + 4,052	31) 8,275 7,920 + 5,769	32) 9,290 6,971 + 5,352

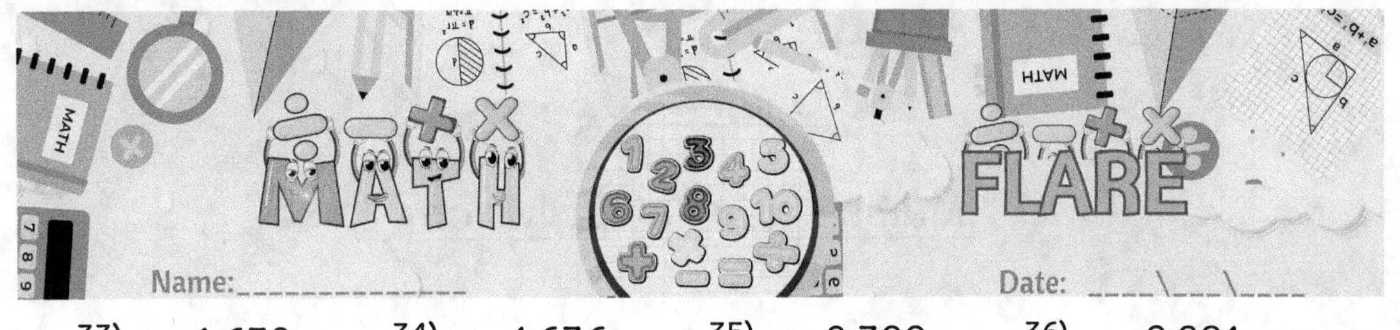

33)   4,639
      3,353
+ 1,523
____

34)   1,636
      1,361
+ 2,720
____

35)   8,399
      8,487
+ 8,923
____

36)   2,291
      6,938
+ 9,284
____

37)   6,727
      8,851
+ 8,888
____

38)   2,195
      8,894
+ 7,531
____

39)   5,895
      9,151
+ 3,794
____

40)   9,277
      2,032
+ 4,754
____

41)   6,382
      7,736
+ 7,199
____

42)   9,736
      3,106
+ 2,195
____

43)   7,781
      3,190
+ 5,748
____

44)   5,250
      1,266
+ 4,327
____

45)   7,517
      7,559
+ 5,373
____

46)   1,488
      3,562
+ 5,532
____

47)   2,023
      9,608
+ 6,235
____

48)   5,512
      8,809
+ 8,297
____

Chapter. 02

Multiplication and Division

Multiplication

Multiplication is an easy way of adding numbers together quickly. Instead of adding the same number repeatedly, we use multiplication to find the total much faster.

For instance, rather than adding 2 + 2 + 2 + 2 + 2, we can multiply 2 by 5 to get the same result: 2 x 5 = 10.

Here, the first number (2) is called the multiplicand, second number (5) is the multiplier. The answer we get, in this case, 10, is called the product.

Let's think of multiplication as repeated addition.

Take 2 x 5, for example. It means adding 2 together five times, which we can illustrate as: 2 + 2 + 2 + 2 + 2 = 10

Multiplication can also be visualized as groups of objects. Imagine we have 2 groups, each containing 5 oranges.

To find the total number of oranges, we multiply the number of groups (2) by the number of oranges in each group (5):

2 groups of 5 oranges = 10 oranges

Expressed as multiplication: 2 x 5 = 10

In summary, multiplication offers various ways to approach it: through repeated addition or by envisioning groups of objects. It's a powerful tool that makes solving math problems much quicker and more efficient!

We can also use the following table to quickly remember multiplication facts. The intersection of two points shows the product of two numbers.

For instance, the product of 5 x 6 = 30, or 6 x 5 = 30.

	1	2	3	4	5	6	7	8	9	10
1	1	2	3	4	5	6	7	8	9	10
2	2	4	6	8	10	12	14	16	18	20
3	3	6	9	12	15	18	21	24	27	30
4	4	8	12	16	20	24	28	32	36	40
5	5	10	15	20	25	30	35	40	45	50
6	6	12	18	24	30	36	42	48	54	60
7	7	14	21	28	35	42	49	56	63	70
8	8	16	24	32	40	48	56	64	72	80
9	9	18	27	36	45	54	63	72	81	90
10	10	20	30	40	50	60	70	80	90	100

Let's solve problems from exercises:

$$
\begin{array}{r}
1{,}202 \\
\times \quad 4 \\
\hline
4{,}808
\end{array}
\qquad
\begin{array}{r}
83 \\
\times \ 86 \\
\hline
498 \\
+664 \\
\hline
7138
\end{array}
\qquad
\begin{array}{r}
552 \\
\times \ 908 \\
\hline
4416 \\
0000 \\
4968 \\
\hline
501216
\end{array}
$$

Division

Division is like the opposite of multiplication. It's all about sharing or distributing items equally among a certain number of groups or people.

When we divide one number by another, we're essentially splitting a number into equal parts. We're figuring out how many groups of a certain size can be made from that number.

For instance, let's divide 20 by 4.

When we divide 20 by 4, we're essentially asking, "How many groups of size 4 can we make from 20?"

Now, there are several parts or terms involved in the division process:

- **Dividend:** This is the number being divided, which in this case, is 20.

- **Divisor:** This is the number we're dividing by, which is 4.

- **Quotient:** This is the answer we get after dividing. It tells us how many groups of divisors can be made from the dividend. In this case, the answer is 5.

So, when we divide 20 by 4, we found out that 5 groups of 4 can be made from 20.

Let's solve problems from exercises:

$$
\begin{array}{r}
4 \\
4\,)\overline{16} \\
-16 \\
\hline
0
\end{array}
\qquad
\begin{array}{r}
42 \\
12\,)\overline{504} \\
-48 \\
\hline
24 \\
-24 \\
\hline
0
\end{array}
\qquad
\begin{array}{r}
477 \\
6\,)\overline{2{,}862} \\
-24 \\
\hline
46 \\
-42 \\
\hline
42 \\
-42 \\
\hline
0
\end{array}
$$

Multiplying Decimals

Multiplying decimals is a lot like multiplying whole numbers, but we need to be careful about where we put the decimal point in the answer.

Step 1: Start by multiplying the numbers together, just like we do with whole numbers. Ignore the decimals for now.

Step 2: Count how many decimal places there are in the numbers we're multiplying. This will tell us how many decimal places our answer should have.

Step 3: Put the decimal point in the answer by starting from the right side of the number. Move the decimal point to the left as many places as there are in the total number of decimal places.

For example, let's multiply 4.5 by 2.5:

Step 1: Multiply the numbers as if they were whole numbers:

$$25 \times 45 = 1125.$$

Step 2: There is one decimal place in 2.5 and one in 4.5, making a total of two decimal places.

Step 3: Starting from the right side of the answer, count two places to the left and put the decimal point there.

So, the final answer is 11.25.

Remember to pay close attention to where the decimal point goes in the answer.

Let's solve a problem:

$$
\begin{array}{r}
22.93 \\
\times \quad 4.69 \\
\hline
+\ 20637 \\
+13758 \\
+9172 \\
\hline
=1075417
\end{array}
$$

Rewrite the product with
4 decimal places.
So the answer is **107.5417**

Dividing Decimals

Dividing decimals is a lot like dividing whole numbers, but we need to be careful about placement of decimal point in the answer.

Steps to follow:

1. **Set up the division problem:** Write the dividend (the number being divided) and the divisor (the number you're dividing by) as you would in a long division problem.

$$1.7\,\overline{)\,1.6}$$

2. **Move the decimal:** Move the decimal point to the right in the dividend and divisor by the same number of places.

$$17\overline{)16}$$

3. **Perform the division:** Divide as you would with whole numbers.

$$
\begin{array}{r}
0\,0.9\,4 \\
17\overline{)16} \\
-\,0 \\
\hline
16 \\
-\,0 \\
\hline
16\,0 \\
-\,15\,3 \\
\hline
7\,0 \\
-\,6\,8 \\
\hline
2
\end{array}
$$

4. **Place the decimal point:** Place the decimal point in the quotient directly above its position in the dividend.

So, the quotient is 0.94.

Long Division with Remainders

Long division with remainders is a method used to divide larger numbers where the divisor doesn't evenly divide the dividend. Let's solve a problem:

$$
\begin{array}{r}
4{,}493 \ \text{R5} \\
14\overline{)62{,}907} \\
56 \\
\hline
69 \\
-\,56 \\
\hline
130 \\
-\,126 \\
\hline
47 \\
-\,42 \\
\hline
5
\end{array}
$$

Using the Power of 10

Using the powers of 10, 100, and 1000 makes multiplying and dividing by these numbers very convenient. Let's illustrate with examples:

Multiplying by Powers of 10:

- To multiply a number by 10, simply move the decimal point one place to the right.

$$5 \times 10 = 50$$

- To multiply a number by 100, move the decimal point two places to the right.

$$5 \times 100 = 500$$

- To multiply a number by 1000, move the decimal point three places to the right.

$$5 \times 1000 = 5000.$$

Dividing by Powers of 10:

- To divide a number by 10, simply move the decimal point one place to the left.

$$50 \div 10 = 5$$

- To divide a number by 100, move the decimal point two places to the left.

$$500 \div 100 = 5$$

- To divide a number by 1000, move the decimal point three places to the left.

$$5000 \div 1000 = 5$$

Using the powers of 10, 100, and 1000 makes multiplying and dividing by these numbers simple and straightforward.

Multiplication and Division Word Problem

Anthony can run four laps in 1 hour. How many laps can Anthony run in 18 hours?

```
    4        1 hour 4 laps
  × 18       how many laps can he  run in 18 hours?
  + 3 2
  + 4
  = 7 2     Anthony can run 72 laps in 18 hours
```

How many 12 cm pieces of rope can you cut from a rope that is 420 cm long?

```
        3 5
   12) 520
      - 36
        60
      - 60
         0
```

35 pieces can be cut

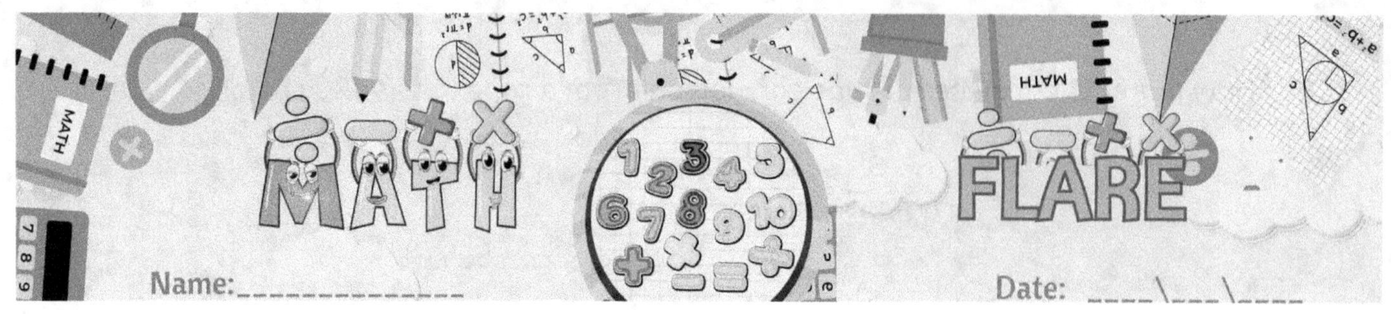

Multiplication (double Digit)

Find the product.

1)
```
    80
  × 93
  -----
   240
   720
 =7440
```

2)
```
    18
  × 87
  -----
```

3)
```
    86
  × 21
  -----
```

4)
```
    65
  × 53
  -----
```

5)
```
    85
  × 70
  -----
```

6)
```
    70
  × 94
  -----
```

7)
```
    86
  × 56
  -----
```

8)
```
    95
  × 94
  -----
```

9)
```
    51
  × 31
  -----
```

10)
```
    45
  × 22
  -----
```

11)
```
    44
  × 31
  -----
```

12)
```
    74
  × 80
  -----
```

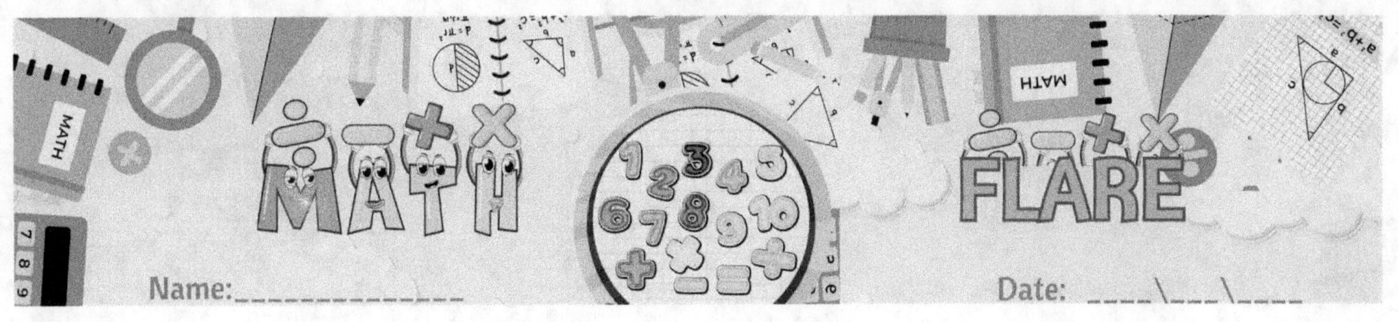

13) 77
× 11
―――

14) 15
× 61
―――

15) 98
× 93
―――

16) 48
× 14
―――

17) 14
× 11
―――

18) 33
× 11
―――

19) 19
× 13
―――

20) 62
× 51
―――

21) 15
× 55
―――

22) 40
× 31
―――

23) 88
× 41
―――

24) 68
× 87
―――

25) 13
× 71
―――

26) 52
× 66
―――

27) 85
× 23
―――

28) 54
× 59
―――

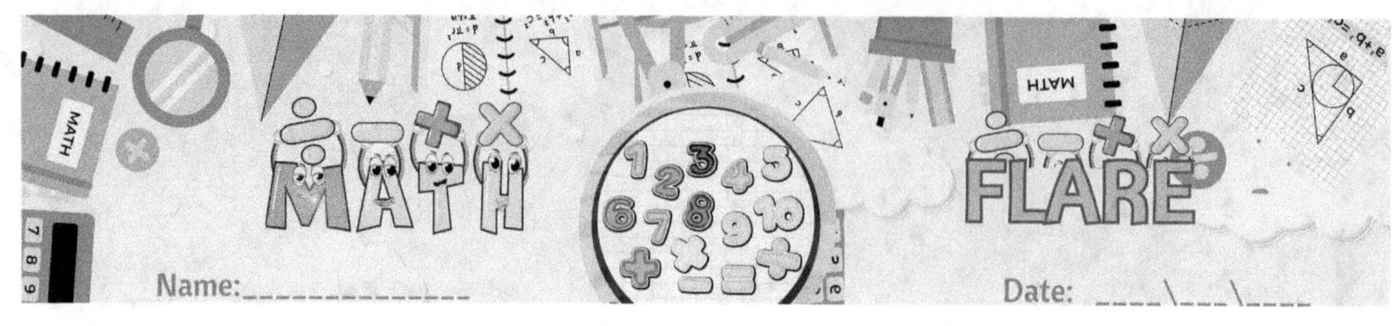

29) 29 × 37	30) 21 × 86	31) 16 × 14	32) 54 × 91
33) 31 × 65	34) 90 × 85	35) 33 × 94	36) 86 × 48
37) 69 × 93	38) 17 × 89	39) 90 × 52	40) 91 × 45
41) 42 × 27	42) 58 × 37	43) 51 × 82	44) 29 × 91

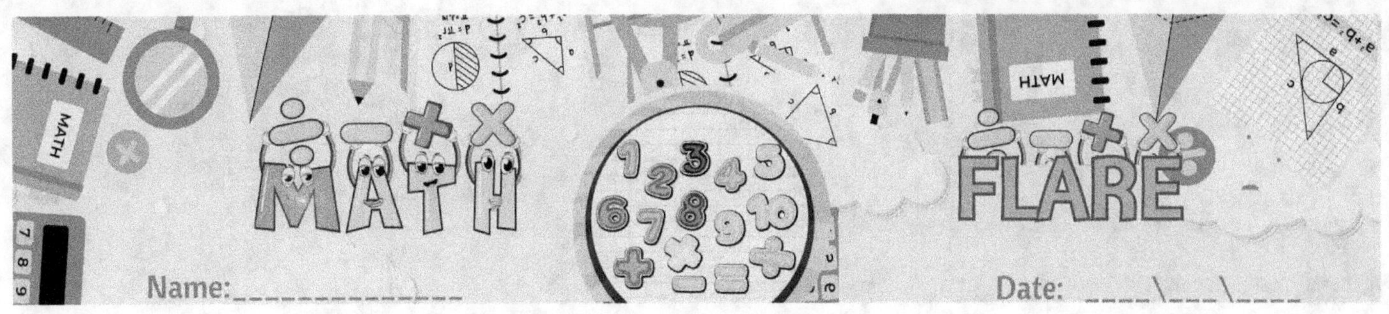

Multiplication (3 Digit)

Find the product.

1) 566
  × 740

  0000
  2264
  3962

  418840

2) 816
  × 818

3) 924
  × 757

4) 455
  × 111

5) 107
  × 489

6) 101
  × 333

7) 511
  × 825

8) 648
  × 180

9) 849
  × 134

10) 972
  × 914

11) 156
  × 647

12) 689
  × 764

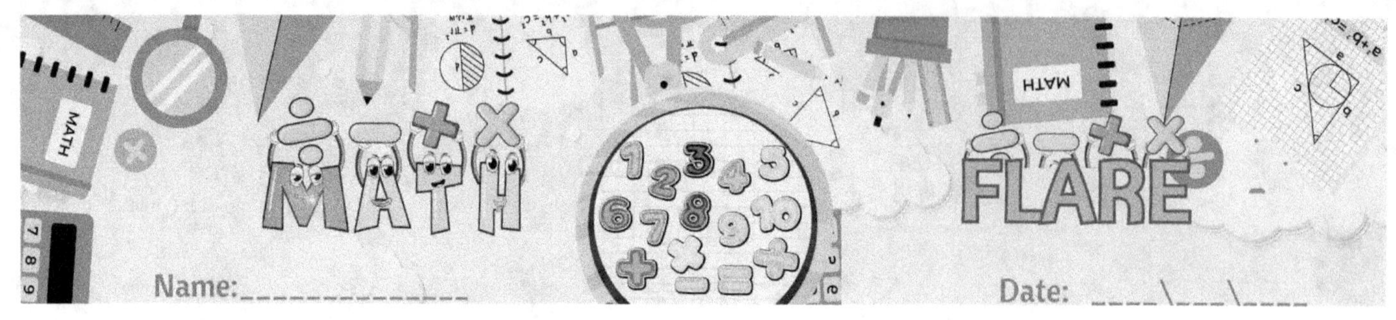

13) 450
   × 748

14) 538
   × 892

15) 549
   × 271

16) 497
   × 491

17) 468
   × 988

18) 389
   × 590

19) 228
   × 148

20) 562
   × 934

21) 582
   × 161

22) 889
   × 516

23) 525
   × 685

24) 946
   × 601

25) 622
   × 509

26) 525
   × 484

27) 849
   × 376

28) 859
   × 919

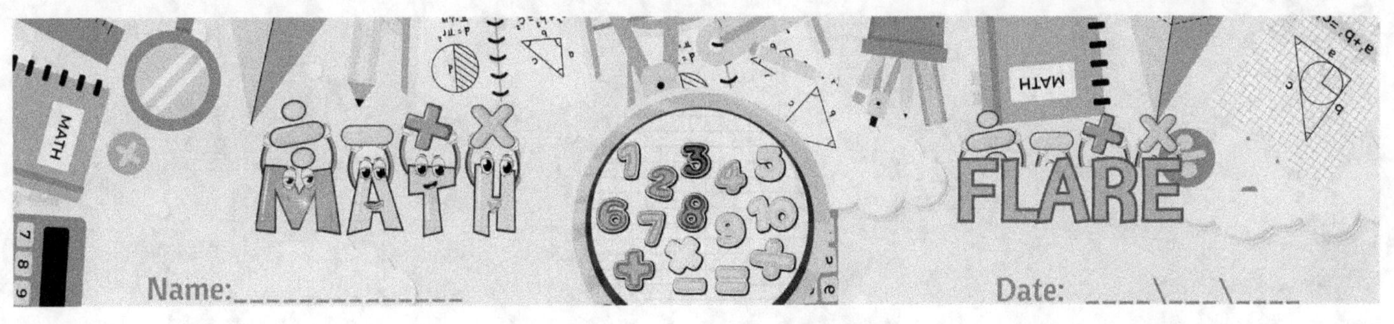

29) 151 × 152	30) 467 × 276	31) 319 × 562	32) 562 × 835
33) 991 × 609	34) 864 × 522	35) 536 × 157	36) 950 × 801
37) 571 × 139	38) 432 × 994	39) 757 × 273	40) 339 × 764
41) 801 × 936	42) 370 × 140	43) 745 × 113	44) 641 × 192

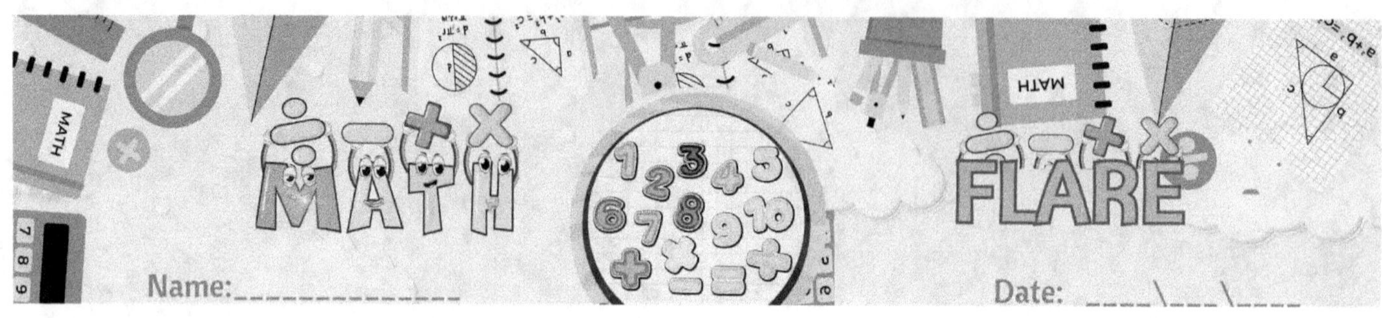

Multiplying Decimals

Find the product.

1) 22.93
  × 4.69

  + 20637
  + 13758
  + 9172
  =1075417

Rewrite the product with
4 decimal places.
So the answer is 107.5417

2) 53.96
  × 1.76

3) 68.00
  × 3.85

4) 71.54
  × 1.20

5) 59.86
  × 1.54

6) 52.48
  × 9.15

7) 82.08
  × 5.24

8) 16.46
  × 5.64

9) 55.81
  × 7.22

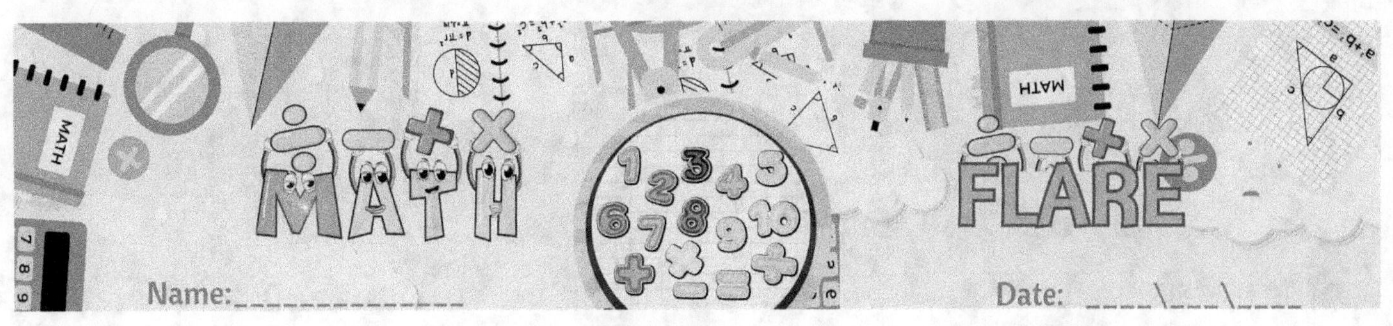

10) 91.30
  × 8.10

11) 94.44
  × 8.64

12) 26.21
  × 8.77

13) 81.32
  × 7.02

14) 47.45
  × 3.82

15) 29.23
  × 5.22

16) 18.94
  × 9.77

17) 96.81
  × 7.72

18) 39.29
  × 1.67

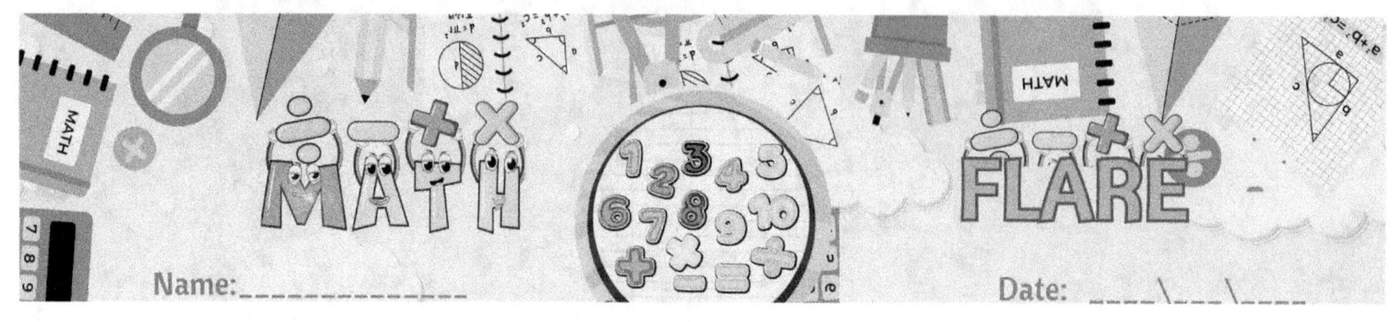

19)   61.78
    × 8.74

20)   22.20
    × 2.85

21)   42.33
    × 4.11

22)   49.64
    × 7.03

23)   74.83
    × 4.23

24)   94.41
    × 3.77

25)   87.25
    × 8.05

26)   58.16
    × 1.23

27)   20.00
    × 8.30

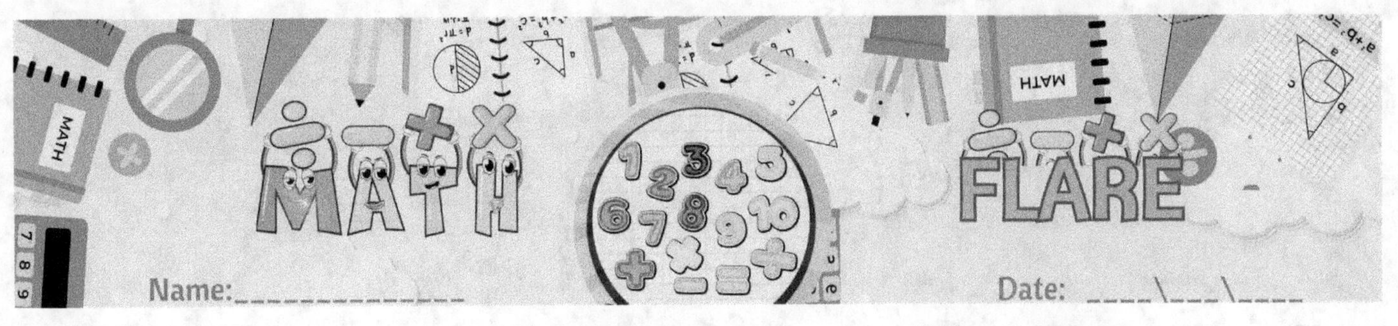

28)

$$24.73 \times 3.65$$

29)

$$30.72 \times 6.61$$

30)

$$36.28 \times 9.76$$

31)

$$91.12 \times 4.33$$

32)

$$82.78 \times 1.76$$

33)

$$96.48 \times 5.46$$

34)

$$94.75 \times 1.48$$

35)

$$23.14 \times 9.96$$

36)

$$94.70 \times 6.82$$

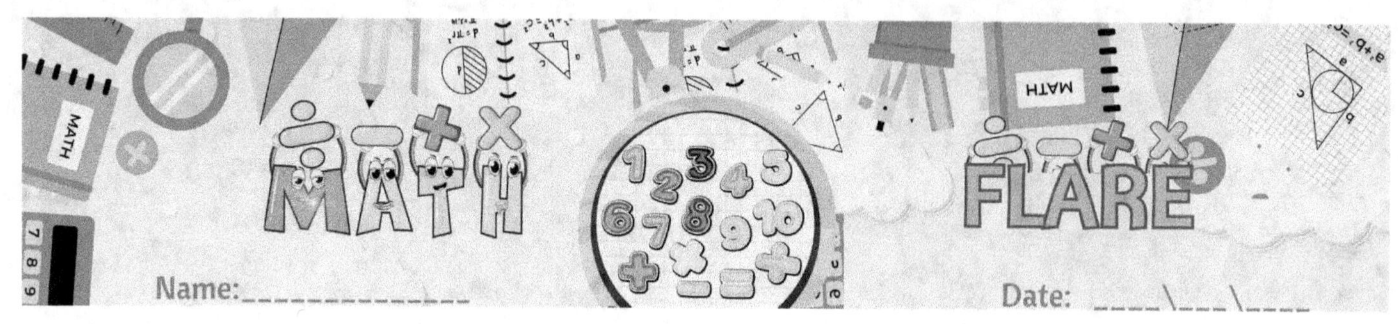

37)   60.10
    ×   7.27
    ____

38)   48.77
    ×   6.32
    ____

39)   46.80
    ×   5.58
    ____

40)   22.94
    ×   4.89
    ____

41)   75.84
    ×   1.97
    ____

42)   50.92
    ×   4.86
    ____

43)   94.06
    ×   1.66
    ____

44)   87.84
    ×   2.37
    ____

45)   62.57
    ×   1.28
    ____

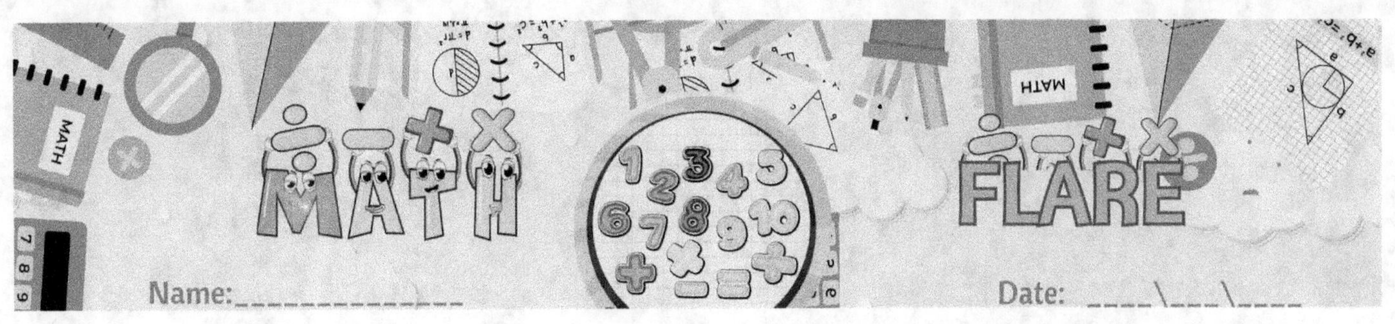

46)   85.99
 ×   9.55

47)   61.23
 ×   2.45

48)   37.44
 ×   9.89

49)   58.38
 ×   4.20

50)   73.82
 ×   3.02

51)   47.57
 ×   8.95

52)   24.60
 ×   8.74

53)   85.84
 ×   8.98

54)   52.18
 ×   4.72

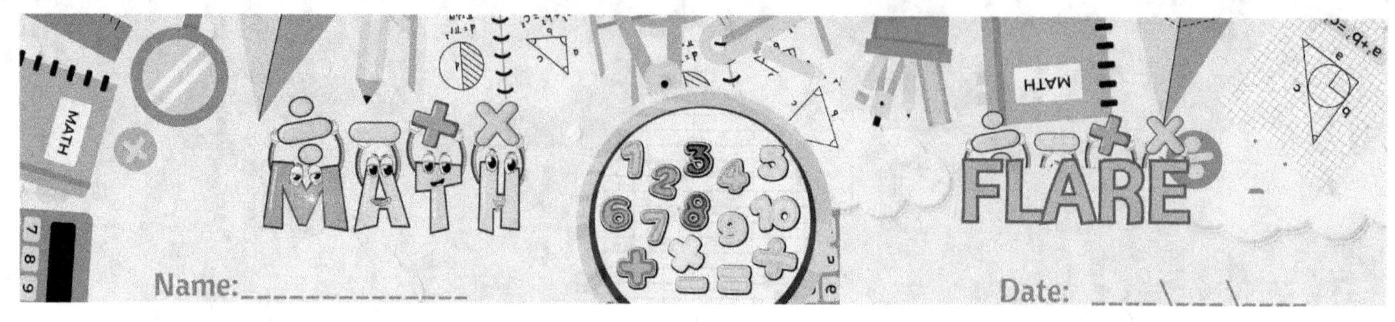

55) 44.28
  × 6.14
______

56) 89.67
  × 7.48
______

57) 53.24
  × 8.72
______

58) 31.88
  × 8.13
______

59) 92.43
  × 4.41
______

60) 23.56
  × 8.97
______

61) 66.78
  × 8.09
______

62) 52.21
  × 2.03
______

63) 23.74
  × 9.90
______

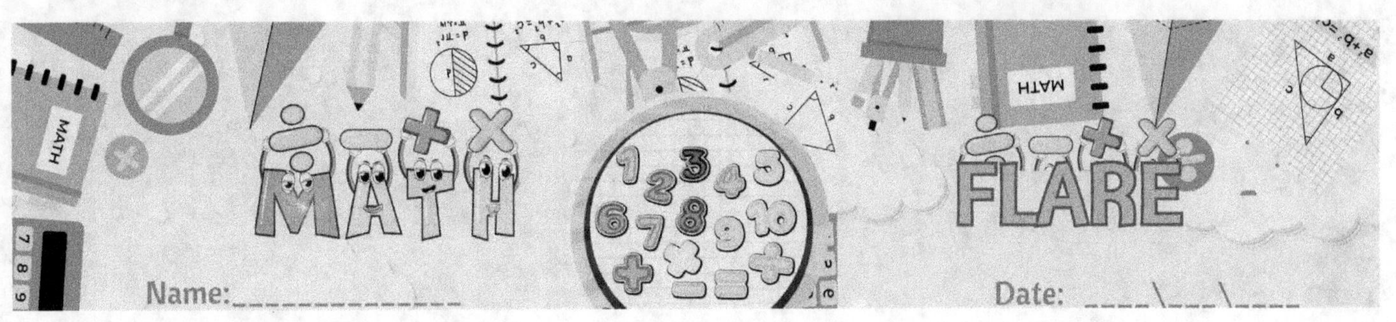

Dividing Decimals
Find the quotient.

1)

$$1.7\overline{)1.6}$$

```
     0 0.9 4
 17 ) 16
    − 0
     16
    − 0
     160
   − 153
       70
      − 68
        2
```

2)

$$4.9\overline{)6.6}$$

3)

$$4.2\overline{)6.9}$$

4)

$$7.7\overline{)7.3}$$

5)

$$3.3\overline{)6.1}$$

6)

$$9.3\overline{)6.1}$$

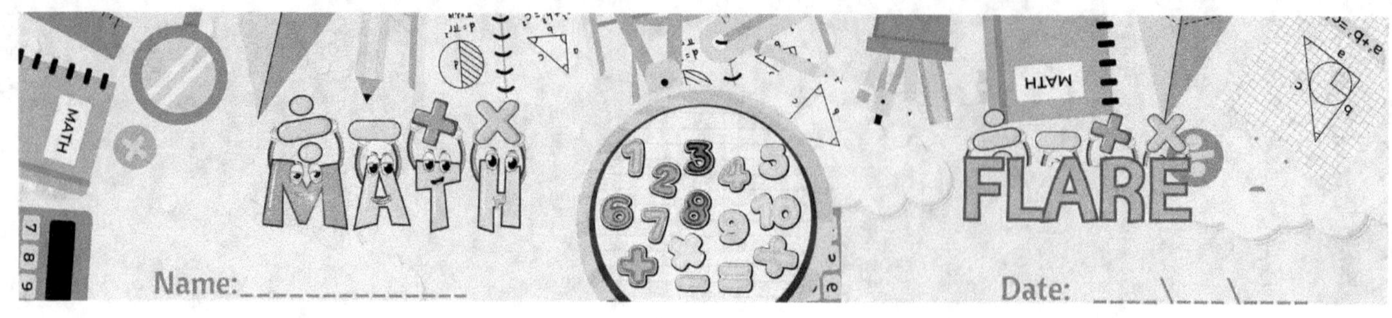

7)

5.7$\overline{)2.0}$

8)

5.2$\overline{)9.5}$

9)

3.2$\overline{)8.8}$

10)

4.9$\overline{)2.7}$

11)

8.9$\overline{)9.7}$

12)

6.7$\overline{)9.2}$

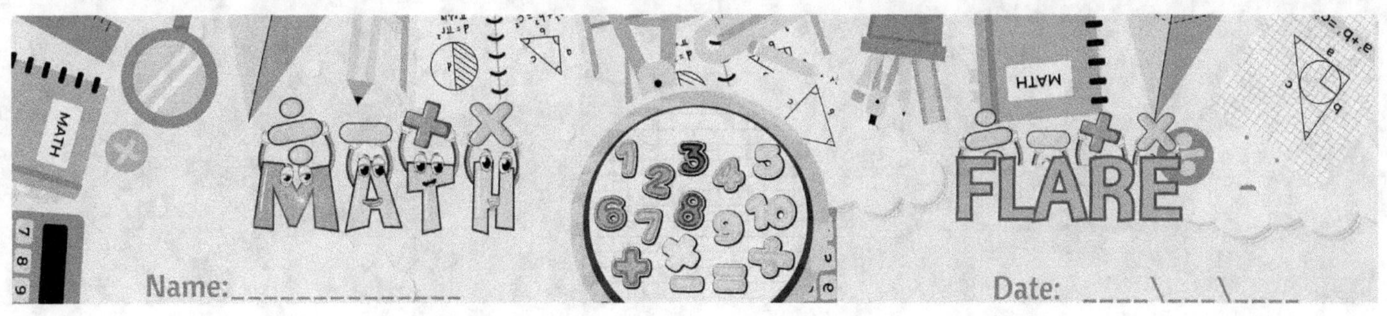

13)

$$4.8 \overline{)6.0}$$

14)

$$2.8 \overline{)1.8}$$

15)

$$5.0 \overline{)1.1}$$

16)

$$3.8 \overline{)5.6}$$

17)

$$4.2 \overline{)7.7}$$

18)

$$8.4 \overline{)8.4}$$

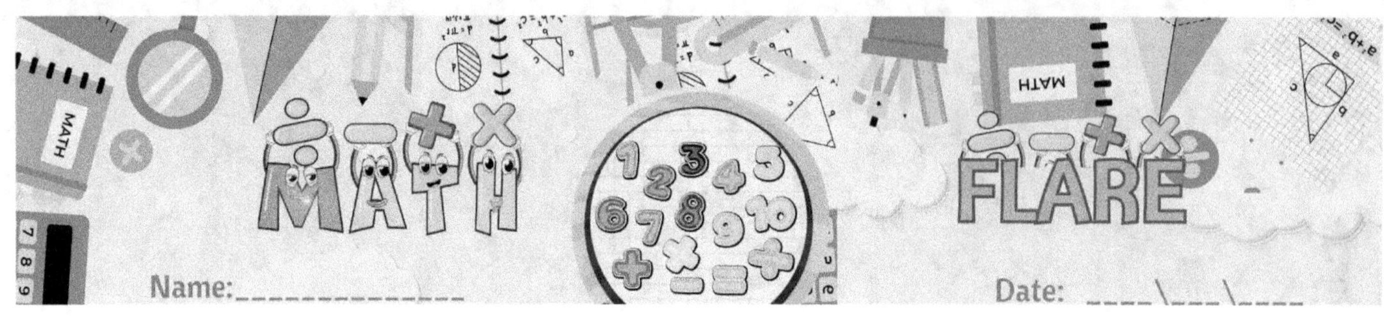

19)

$$3.8\overline{)1.1}$$

20)

$$8.5\overline{)8.2}$$

21)

$$5.4\overline{)9.3}$$

22)

$$9.7\overline{)3.5}$$

23)

$$3.6\overline{)2.2}$$

24)

$$4.6\overline{)7.8}$$

25)

4.5)‾4.7‾

26)

3.3)‾1.5‾

27)

5.5)‾4.3‾

28)

2.6)‾5.3‾

29)

9.9)‾2.3‾

30)

3.1)‾8.8‾

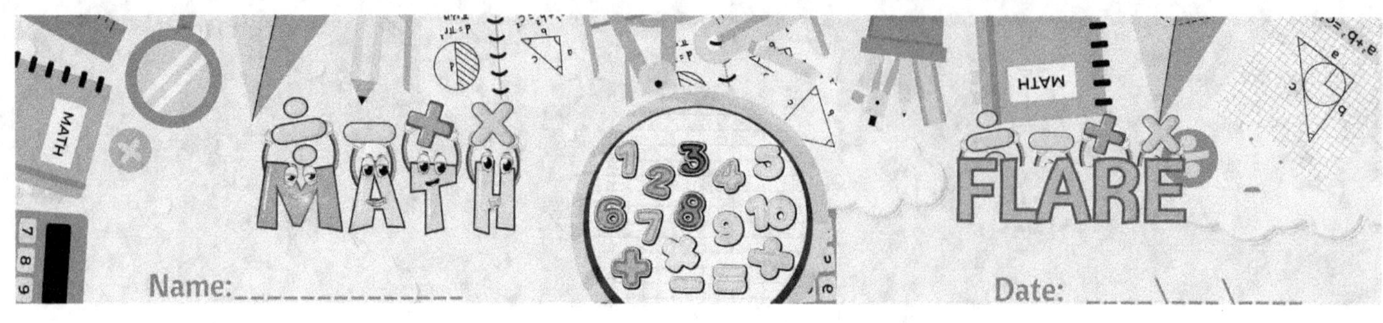

31)

$$5.5\overline{)3.4}$$

32)

$$2.1\overline{)7.6}$$

33)

$$3.3\overline{)7.6}$$

34)

$$7.7\overline{)2.7}$$

35)

$$2.1\overline{)7.2}$$

36)

$$5.9\overline{)5.1}$$

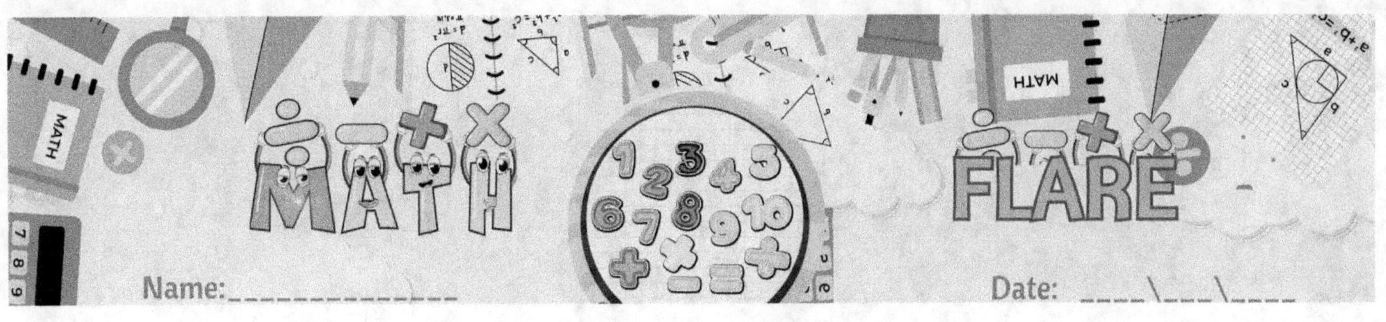

37)

$4.0\overline{)4.8}$

38)

$5.3\overline{)5.5}$

39)

$9.5\overline{)6.4}$

40)

$3.4\overline{)5.5}$

41)

$7.1\overline{)6.9}$

42)

$6.5\overline{)8.0}$

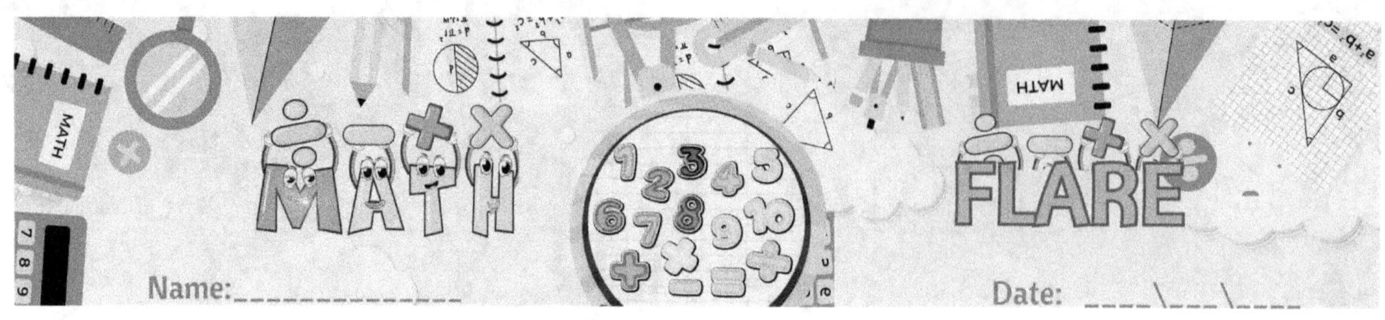

Long Division: Remainders

Find the quotient.

1)
$$14 \overline{)62{,}907} \quad 4{,}493 \text{ R5}$$

```
        4,493 R5
    14) 62,907
        56
        69
       -56
        130
       -126
         47
        -42
          5
```

2)
$$13 \overline{)62{,}705}$$

3)
$$8 \overline{)21{,}101}$$

4)
$$3 \overline{)21{,}841}$$

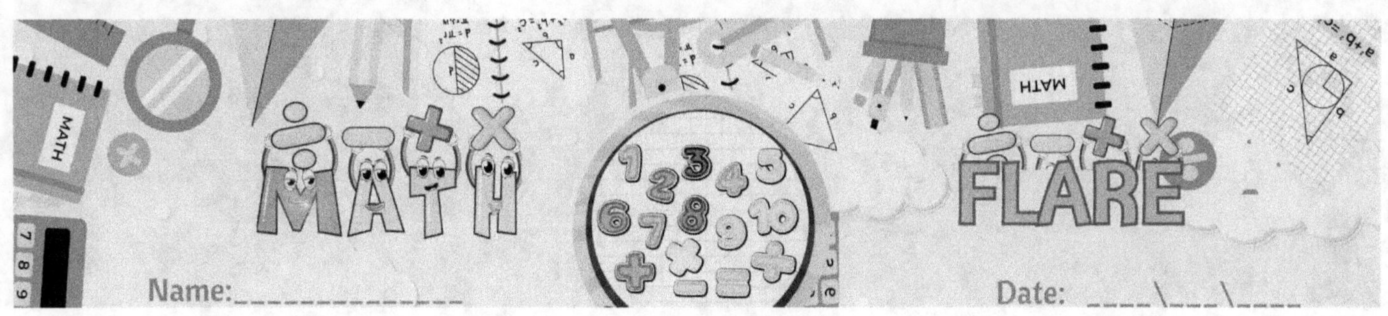

5)

$12 \overline{)33{,}697}$

6)

$19 \overline{)64{,}250}$

7)

$11 \overline{)57{,}774}$

8)

$10 \overline{)65{,}593}$

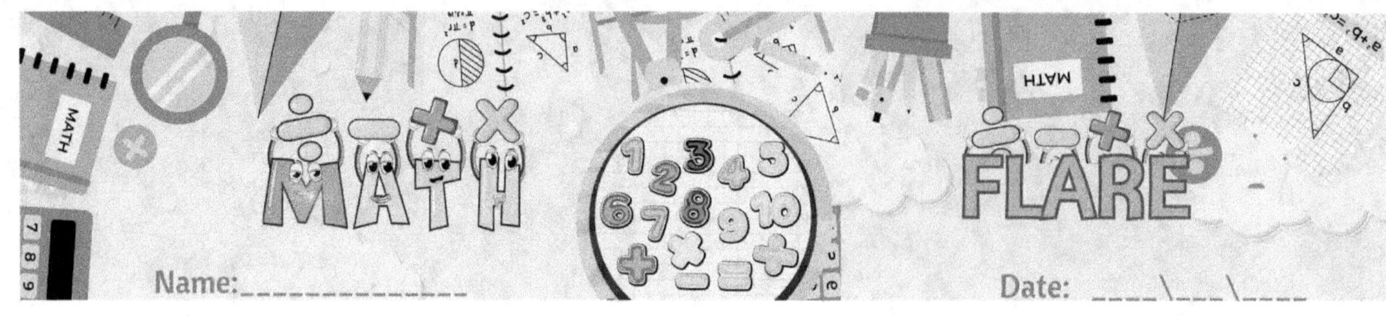

9)

6) 15,130

10)

4) 35,542

11)

14) 54,834

12)

18) 83,552

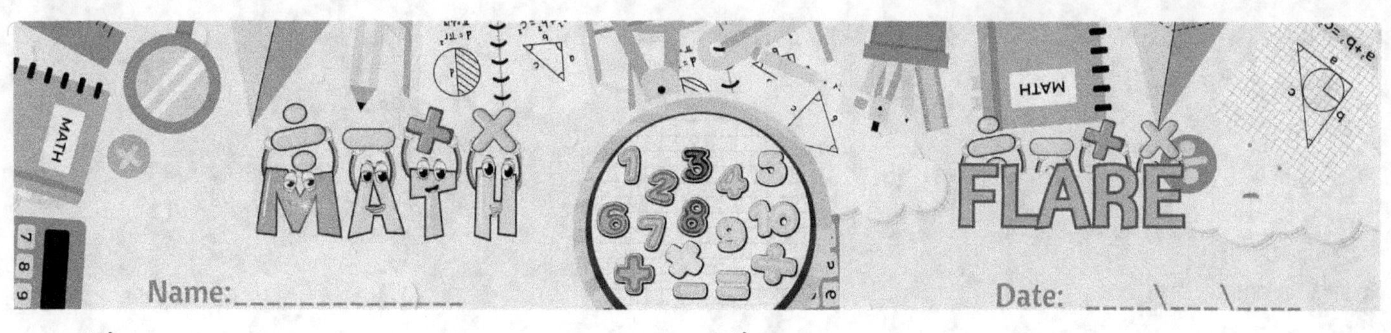

13)

$$17 \overline{)\,30{,}384}$$

14)

$$19 \overline{)\,81{,}155}$$

15)

$$3 \overline{)\,12{,}171}$$

16)

$$7 \overline{)\,95{,}378}$$

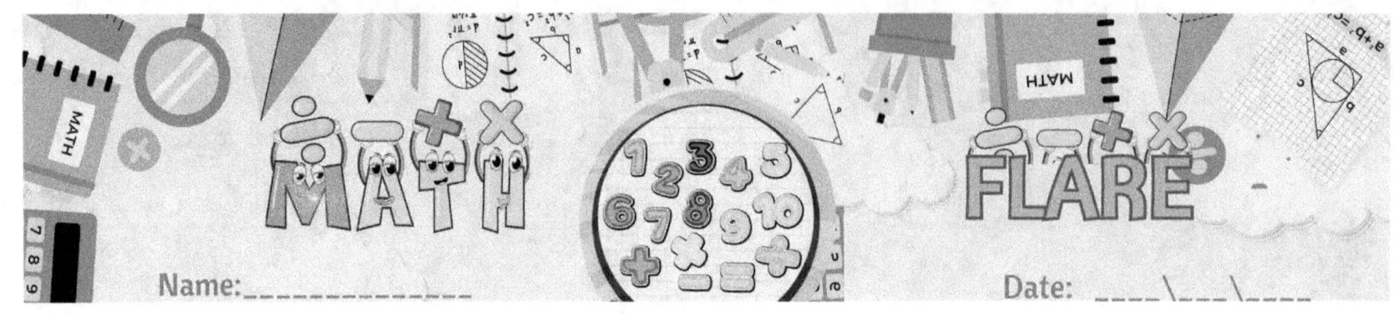

17)

$$19 \overline{)35{,}596}$$

18)

$$13 \overline{)50{,}061}$$

19)

$$15 \overline{)56{,}512}$$

20)

$$16 \overline{)70{,}679}$$

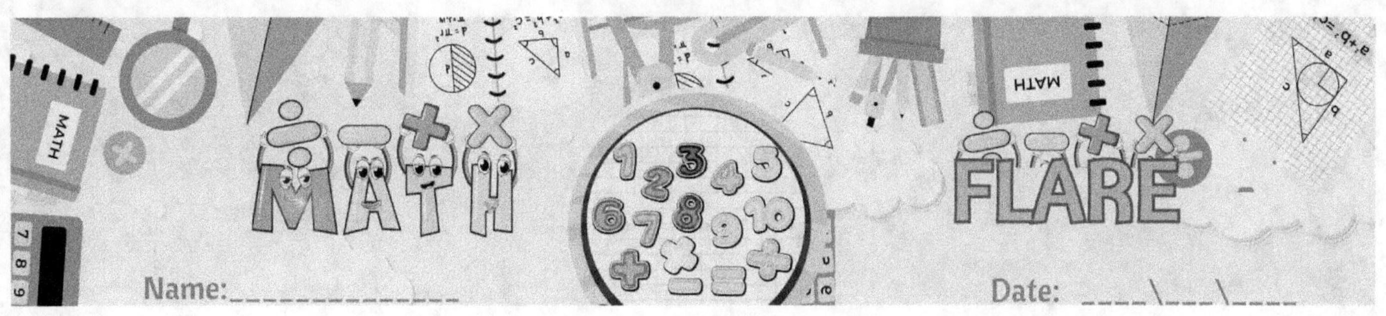

21)

19) 34,645

22)

8) 32,960

23)

9) 84,220

24)

13) 83,807

25)

$$9\overline{)27{,}000}$$

26)

$$8\overline{)27{,}169}$$

27)

$$12\overline{)50{,}630}$$

28)

$$19\overline{)31{,}453}$$

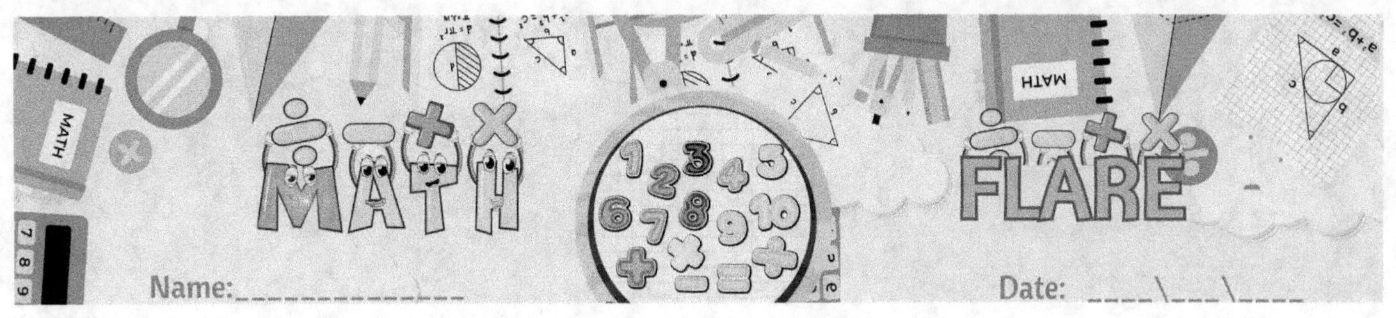

Using the Power of 10

1)
$$1{,}000 \times 10 = 10{,}000$$

2)
$$3{,}000 \times 1{,}000$$

3)
$$3{,}000 \times 1{,}000$$

4)
$$5{,}000 \times 10$$

5)
$$1{,}000 \overline{)\, 5{,}000}$$

6)
$$1{,}000 \times 10$$

7)
$$100 \overline{)\, 7{,}000}$$

8)
$$4{,}000 \times 100$$

9)
$$4{,}000 \times 10$$

10)
$$10 \overline{)\, 3{,}000}$$

11)
$$2{,}000 \times 100$$

12)
$$7{,}000 \times 10$$

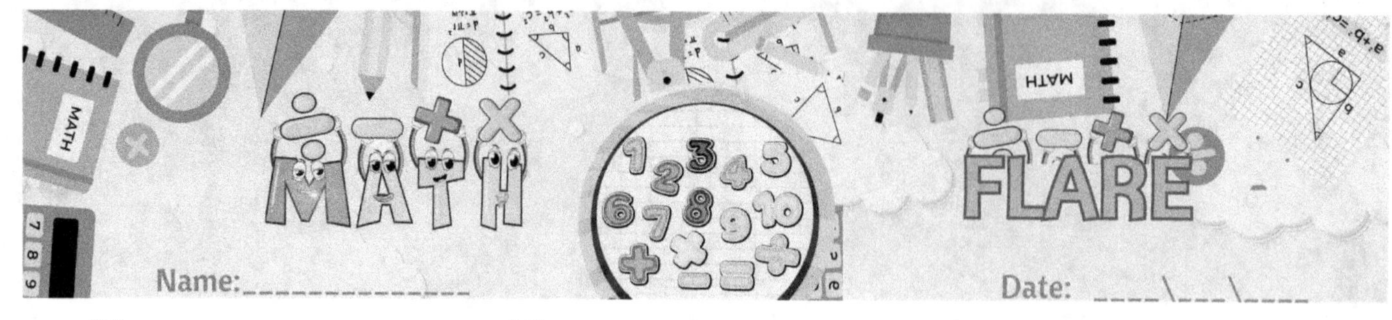

13) $\begin{array}{r} 1,000 \\ \times\quad 100 \\ \hline \end{array}$

14) $10\overline{)7,000}$

15) $10\overline{)3,000}$

16) $\begin{array}{r} 6,000 \\ \times\quad 10 \\ \hline \end{array}$

17) $10\overline{)5,000}$

18) $1,000\overline{)8,000}$

19) $10\overline{)2,000}$

20) $100\overline{)7,000}$

21) $\begin{array}{r} 8,000 \\ \times\quad 100 \\ \hline \end{array}$

22) $1,000\overline{)2,000}$

23) $100\overline{)6,000}$

24) $\begin{array}{r} 9,000 \\ \times\quad 10 \\ \hline \end{array}$

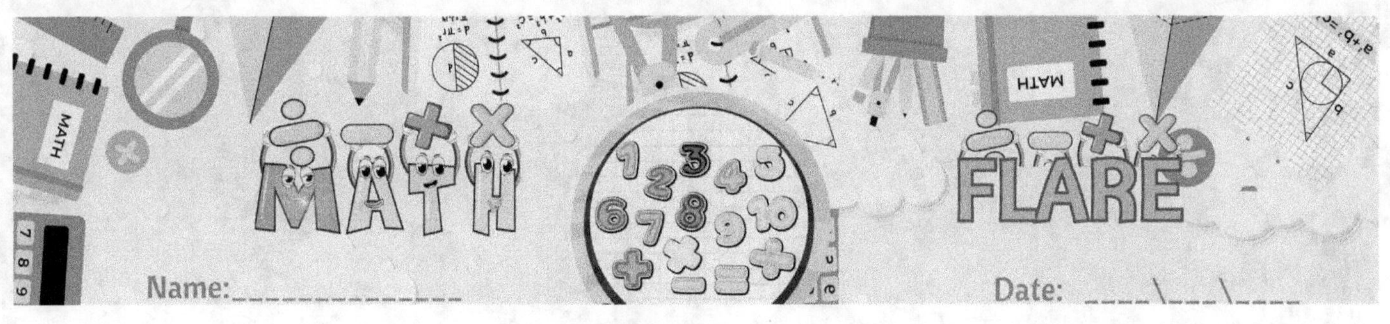

25)

100)9,000

26)

3,000
× 1,000

27)

1,000)1,000

28)

1,000)6,000

29)

10)9,000

30)

1,000)4,000

31)

100)3,000

32)

10)1,000

33)

7,000
× 10

34)

8,000
× 1,000

35)

1,000)8,000

36)

10)3,000

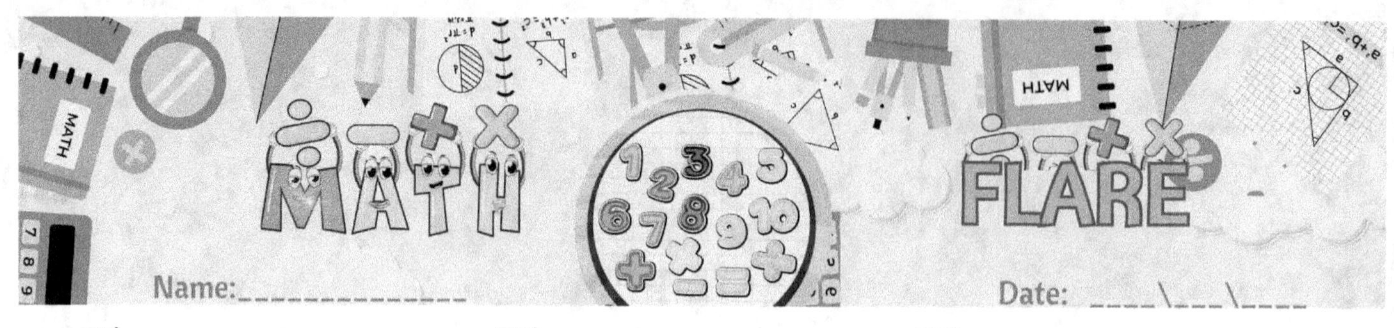

37) 3,000
   × 1,000
   ⎯⎯⎯⎯⎯

38) 2,000
   × 1,000
   ⎯⎯⎯⎯⎯

39) 7,000
   × 1,000
   ⎯⎯⎯⎯⎯

40) 1,000) 4,000

41) 5,000
   ×   100
   ⎯⎯⎯⎯⎯

42) 100) 2,000

43) 2,000
   ×   10
   ⎯⎯⎯⎯⎯

44) 6,000
   × 1,000
   ⎯⎯⎯⎯⎯

45) 100) 5,000

46) 9,000
   ×   100
   ⎯⎯⎯⎯⎯

47) 7,000
   × 1,000
   ⎯⎯⎯⎯⎯

48) 9,000
   ×   10
   ⎯⎯⎯⎯⎯

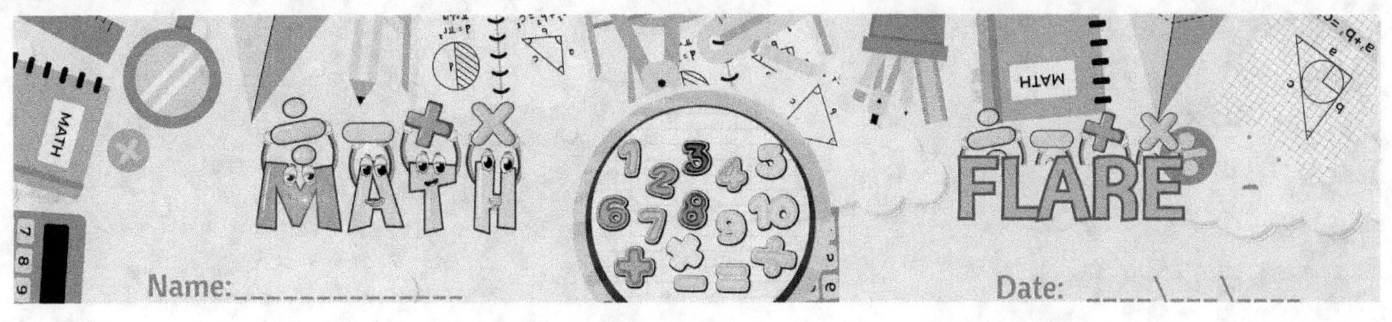

49)

$$100 \overline{) 2{,}000}$$

50)

$$\begin{array}{r} 1{,}000 \\ \times \quad 10 \\ \hline \end{array}$$

51)

$$100 \overline{) 8{,}000}$$

52)

$$10 \overline{) 6{,}000}$$

53)

$$\begin{array}{r} 1{,}000 \\ \times \quad 100 \\ \hline \end{array}$$

54)

$$1{,}000 \overline{) 2{,}000}$$

55)

$$\begin{array}{r} 3{,}000 \\ \times \quad 10 \\ \hline \end{array}$$

56)

$$10 \overline{) 9{,}000}$$

57)

$$100 \overline{) 6{,}000}$$

58)

$$\begin{array}{r} 4{,}000 \\ \times \quad 1{,}000 \\ \hline \end{array}$$

59)

$$\begin{array}{r} 5{,}000 \\ \times \quad 1{,}000 \\ \hline \end{array}$$

60)

$$10 \overline{) 3{,}000}$$

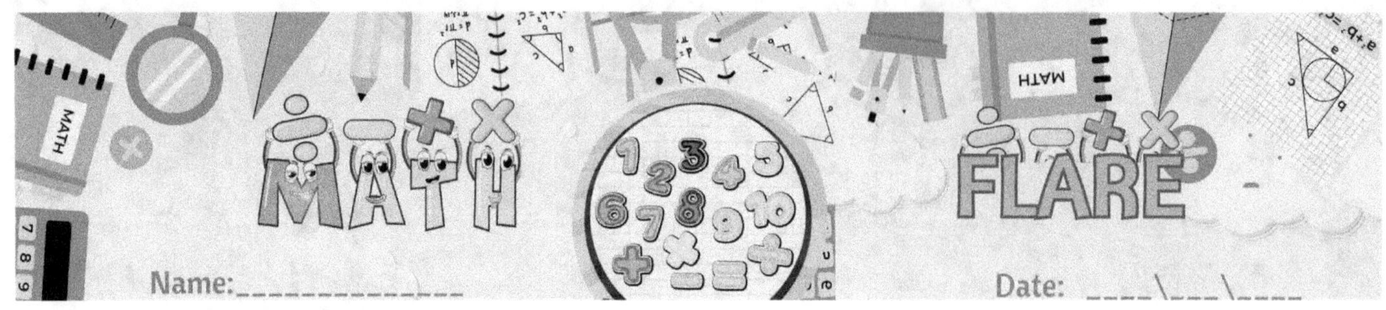

Multiplication Word Problems

1) There are four shelves in Asher's bookcase. Six books can fit on each shelf. How many books can the bookcase hold in total?

$$\begin{array}{r} 4 \\ \times\ 6 \\ \hline 24 \end{array}$$

4 shelf in bookcase
6 books in each shelf
bookcase can hold 24 books.

2) If a boat travels at 11 miles per hour for three hours, how far will it go?

3) Jose earns 14 dollars per hour. How much will Jose earn after working for six hours?

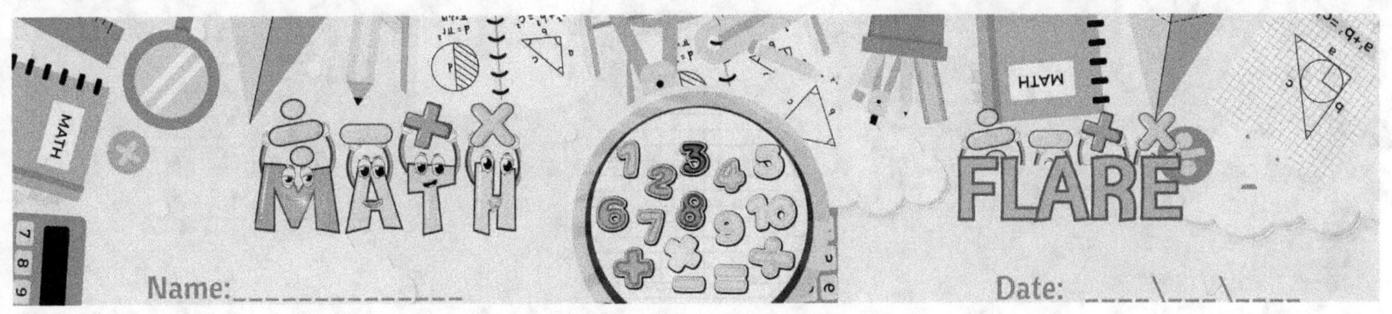

4) A recipe for a cake calls for five cups of flour. How many cups of flour are needed to make two cakes?

5) If a car travels at 14 miles per hour for seven hours, how far will it go?

6) A movie theater can seat seven people. How many people can it seat in 16 showings?

7) Brody can do 10 pushups in one minute. How many pushups can Brody do in 15 minutes?

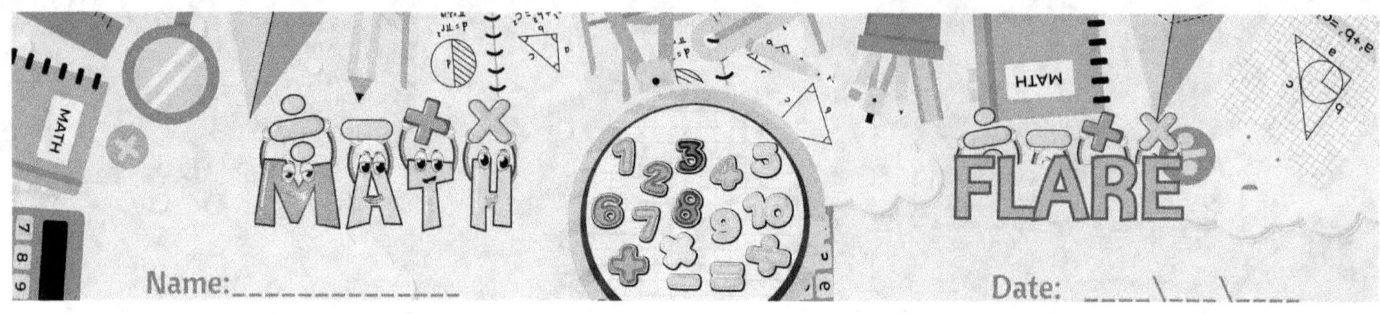

8) Wyatt can lift 19 pounds of weight. How many pounds of weight can Wyatt lift in total if he lifts for 16 sets?

9) Michael runs six miles every day. How many miles will Michael run in 20 days?

10) A bookshelf can hold four books. If there are 14 bookshelves in a room, how many books can the room hold in total?

11) A garden has 17 rows of flowers and 12 flowers in each row. How many flowers are there in total?

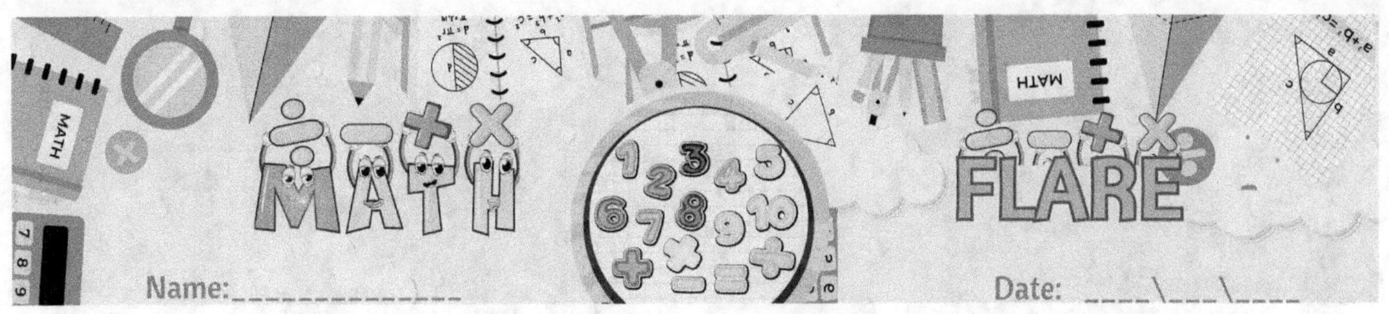

12) Adalyn baked eight batches of cookies. Each batch had 14 cookies. How many cookies did Adalyn bake in all?

13) David can solve 10 math problems in one hour. How many problems can David solve in 18 hours?

14) Ryder can ride four miles in one hour. How far can he ride in 19 hours?

15) Aubrey has 19 jars of jam. Each jar has seven ounces of jam. How many ounces of jam does Aubrey have in all?

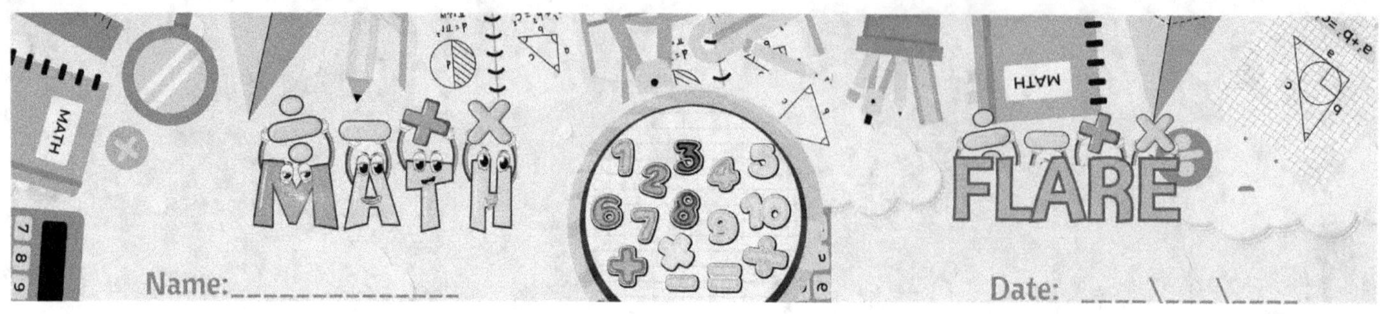

16) If Cooper can paint three square feet of wall in one hour, how many square feet of wall can he paint in 11 hours?

17) If a bicycle travels at 18 miles per hour for eight hours, how far will it go?

18) If there are 18 students in each classroom and there are five classrooms, how many students are there in total?

19) There are 18 shelves in a library. 13 books can fit on each shelf. How many books the library have in total?

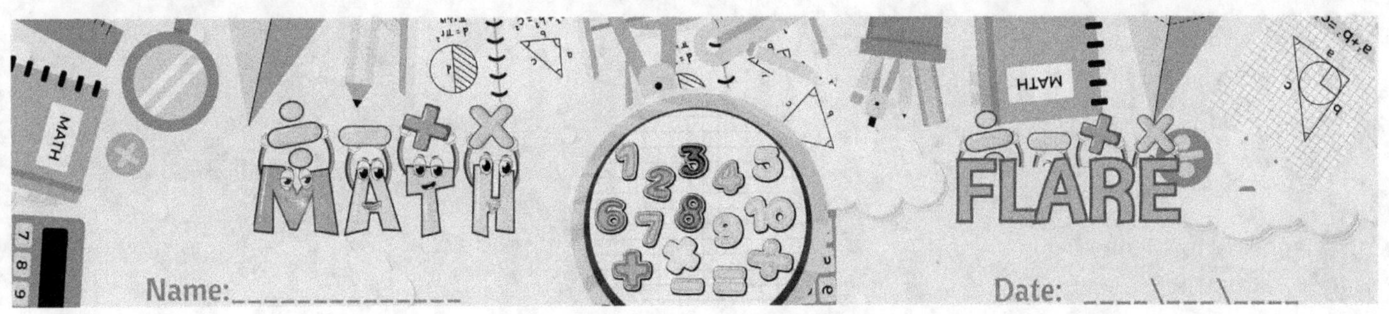

20) Leah has 18 boxes of cotton swabs. Each box has eight cotton swabs. How many cotton swabs does Leah have in all?

21) There are 20 pencils in each pack. If Genesis buys nine packs, how many pencils will Genesis have?

22) There are three flowers in each bouquet. If Emma has 19 bouquets, how many flowers does Emma have in all?

23) Miles can solve 11 math problems in one hour. How many math problems can Miles solve in two hours?

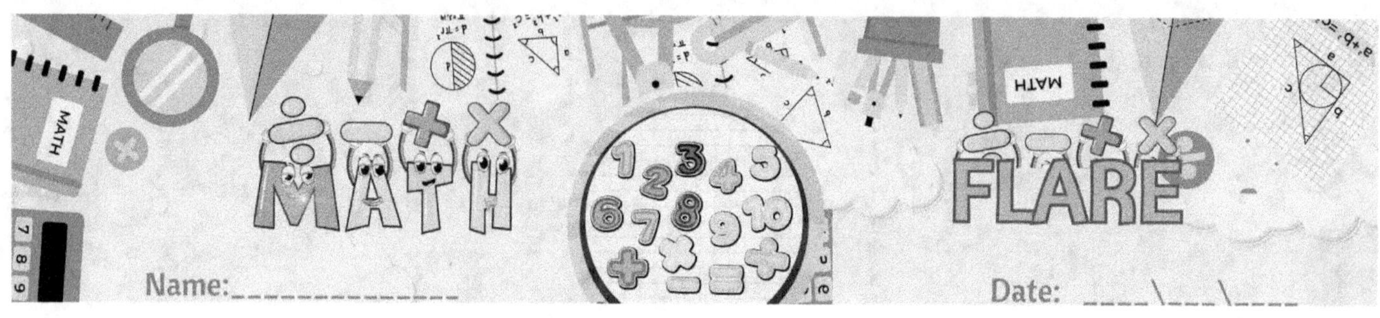

24) Joshua can lift four pounds of weight. How many pounds of weight can he lift in 12 repetitions?

25) There are 15 seats on a bus. If 10 buses are needed to transport a group of people, how many people can the group consist of at most?

26) Aiden runs 18 miles per week. How many miles will Aiden run in 20 weeks?

27) Miles sells 17 cakes each day at his bakery. If he works 18 days, how many cakes does he sell?

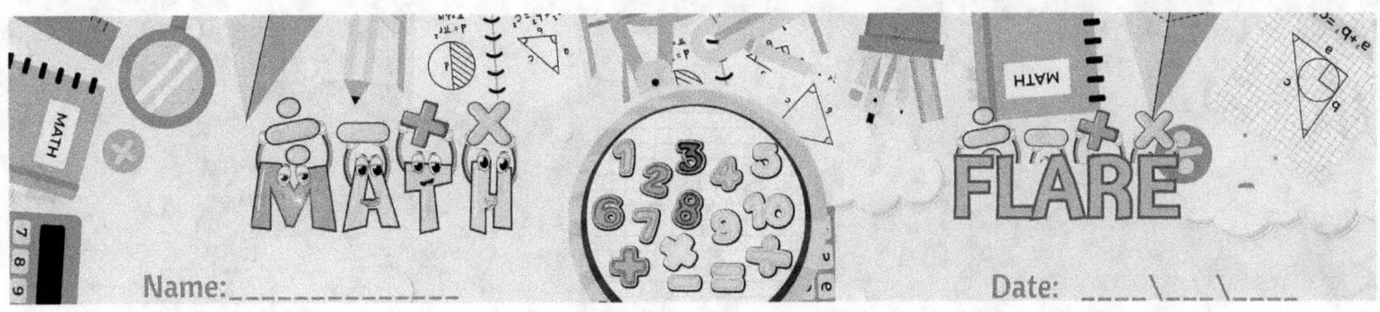

28) There are 14 students in a class. If each student needs 12 pencils, how many pencils are needed for the class in total?

29) Daniel can type 19 words per minute. How many words can Daniel type in 18 minutes?

30) Penelope has 14 books on each shelf, and there are 16 shelves. How many books does Penelope have in total?

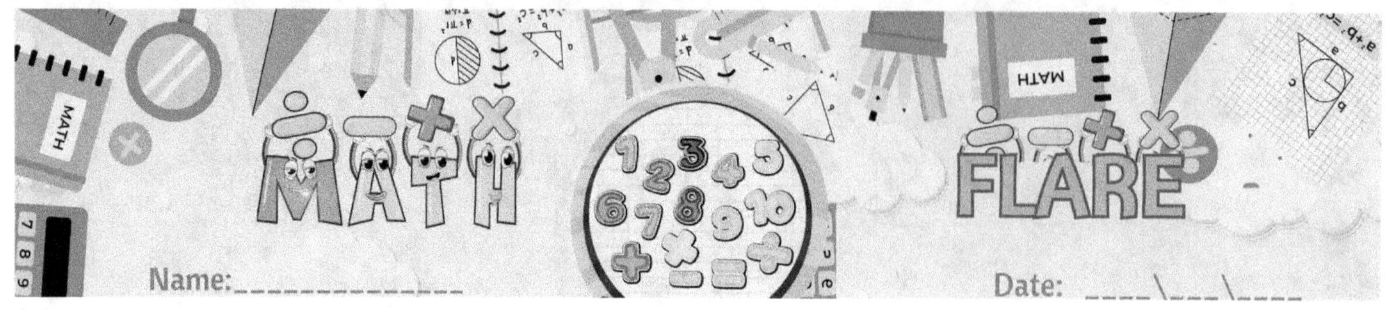

Division Word Problems

1) Audrey made 472 cookies for a bake sale. She put the cookies in bags, with eight cookies in each bag. How many bags did she have for the bake sale?

2) Adam ordered 17 pizzas. The bill for the pizzas came to $408. What was the cost of each pizza?

3) David is reading a book with 975 pages. If David wants to read the same number of pages every day, how many pages would David have to read each day to finish in 13 days?

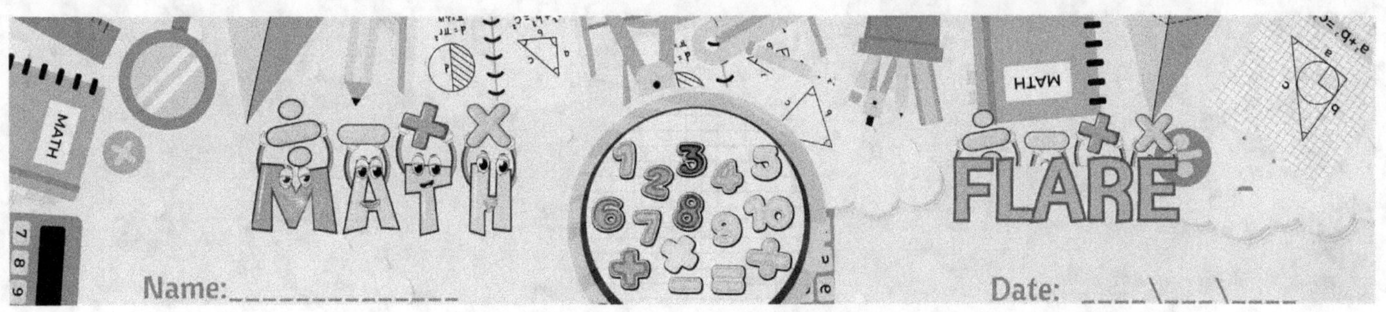

4) A box of oranges weighs 1,500 pounds. If one orange weighs 15 pounds, how many oranges are there in the box?

5) How many 13 cm pieces of rope can you cut from a rope that is 871 cm long?

6) You have 336 apples and want to share them equally with 12 people. How many apples would each person get?

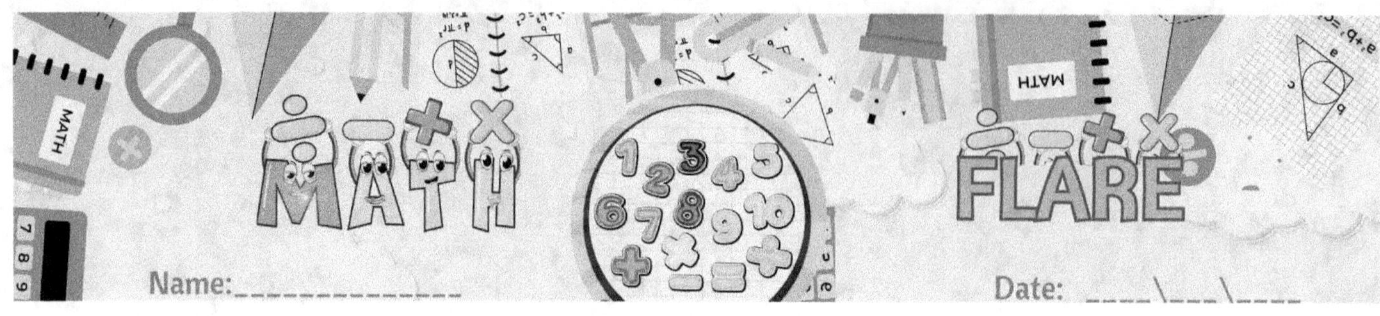

7) Brian is reading a book with 574 pages. If Brian wants to read the same number of pages every day, how many pages would Brian have to read each day to finish in seven days?

8) How many eight cm pieces of rope can you cut from a rope that is 712 cm long?

9) A box of oranges weighs 602 pounds. If one orange weighs seven pounds, how many oranges are there in the box?

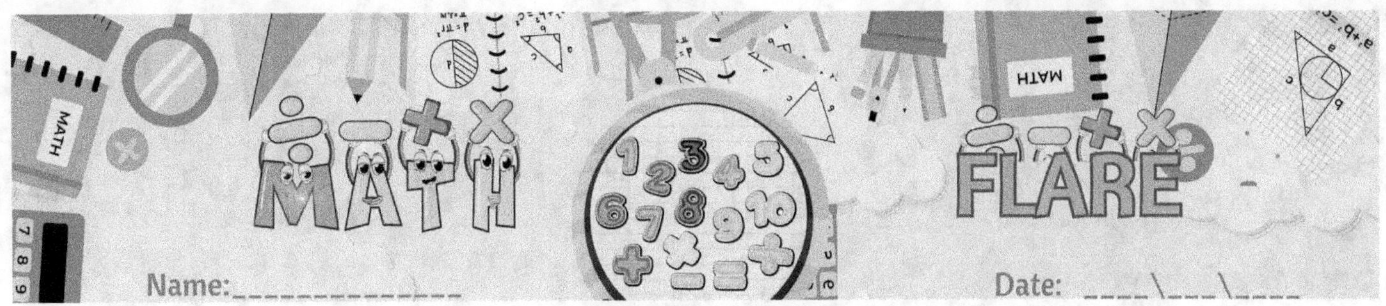

10) You have 133 mangoes and want to share them equally with 19 people. How many mangoes would each person get?

11) Brian ordered nine pizzas. The bill for the pizzas came to $225. What was the cost of each pizza?

12) Sandra made 432 cookies for a bake sale. She put the cookies in bags, with 12 cookies in each bag. How many bags did she have for the bake sale?

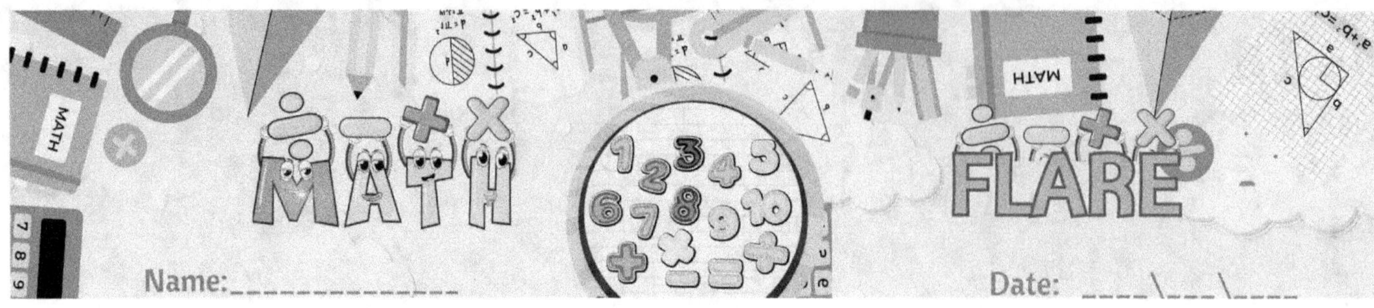

13) How many 10 cm pieces of rope can you cut from a rope that is 270 cm long?

14) Amy made 1,020 cookies for a bake sale. She put the cookies in bags, with 12 cookies in each bag. How many bags did she have for the bake sale?

15) You have 1,400 bananas and want to share them equally with 20 people. How many bananas would each person get?

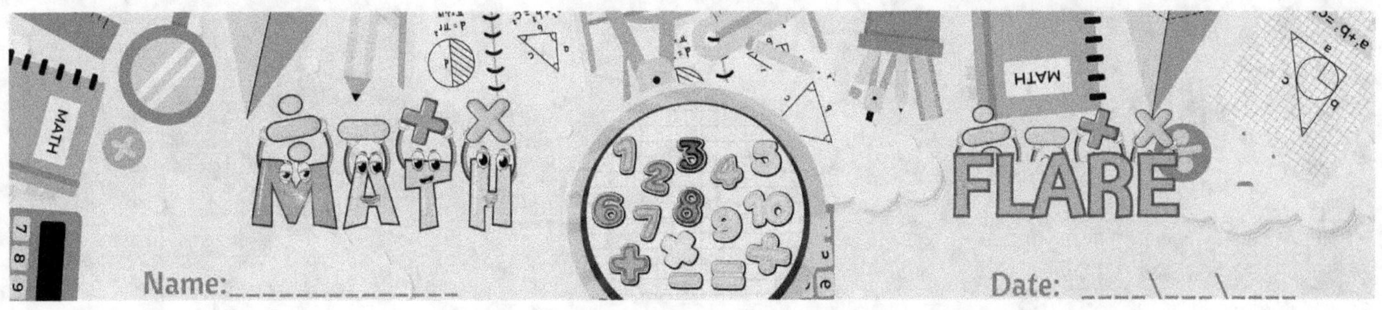

16) A box of pears weighs 300 pounds. If one pear weighs 12 pounds, how many pears are there in the box?

17) Paul is reading a book with 320 pages. If Paul wants to read the same number of pages every day, how many pages would Paul have to read each day to finish in 20 days?

18) Amy ordered 11 pizzas. The bill for the pizzas came to $99. What was the cost of each pizza?

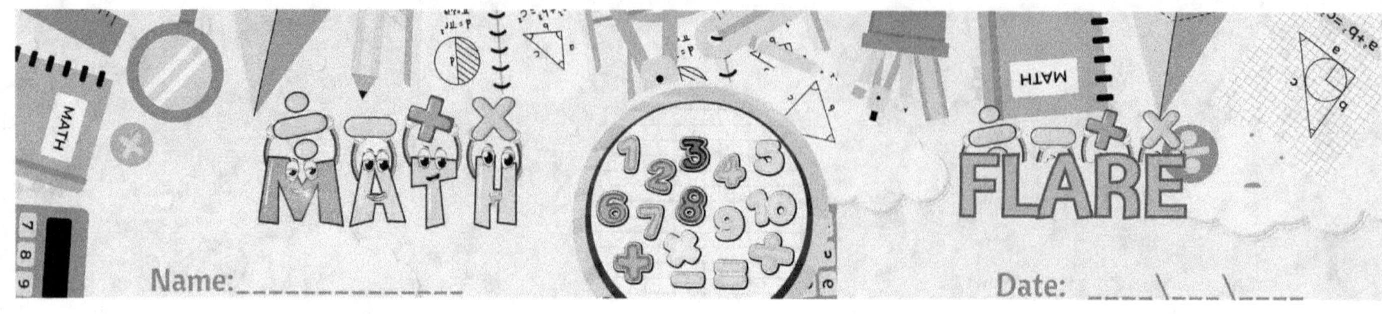

Name:______________________   Date: ____________

19) You have 1,296 peaches and want to share them equally with 18 people. How many peaches would each person get?

20) Janet ordered six pizzas. The bill for the pizzas came to $294. What was the cost of each pizza?

21) Jennifer made 504 cookies for a bake sale. She put the cookies in bags, with nine cookies in each bag. How many bags did she have for the bake sale?

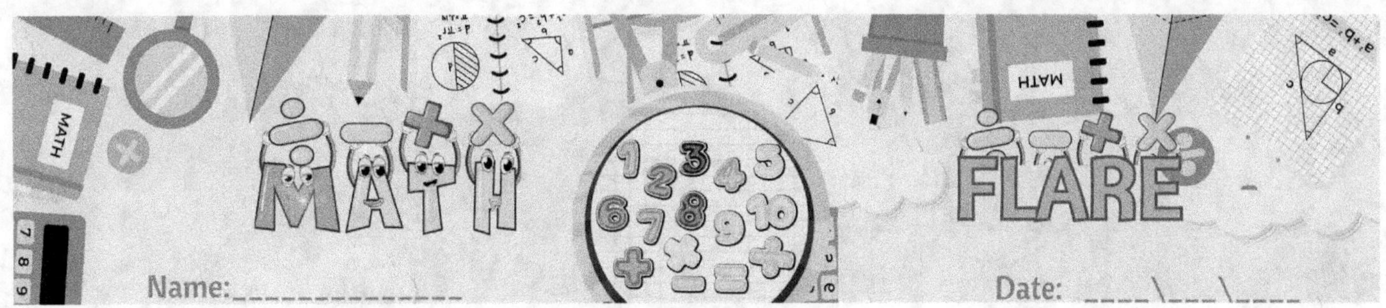

Name:_______________   Date: ____________

22) How many six cm pieces of rope can you cut from a rope that is 108 cm long?

23) Jake is reading a book with 144 pages. If Jake wants to read the same number of pages every day, how many pages would Jake have to read each day to finish in nine days?

24) A box of plums weighs 276 pounds. If one plum weighs six pounds, how many plums are there in the box?

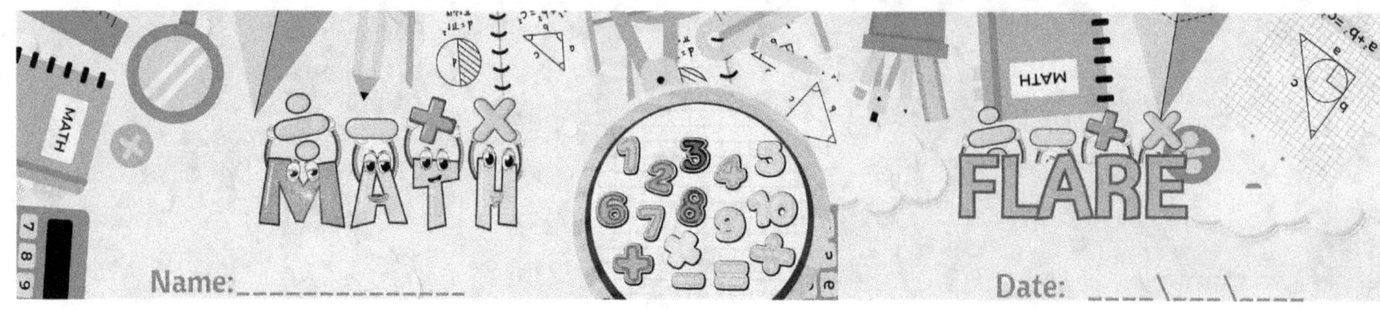

25) A box of mangoes weighs 15 pounds. If one mango weighs three pounds, how many mangoes are there in the box?

26) Sharon ordered 16 pizzas. The bill for the pizzas came to $752. What was the cost of each pizza?

27) Jake is reading a book with 774 pages. If Jake wants to read the same number of pages every day, how many pages would Jake have to read each day to finish in nine days?

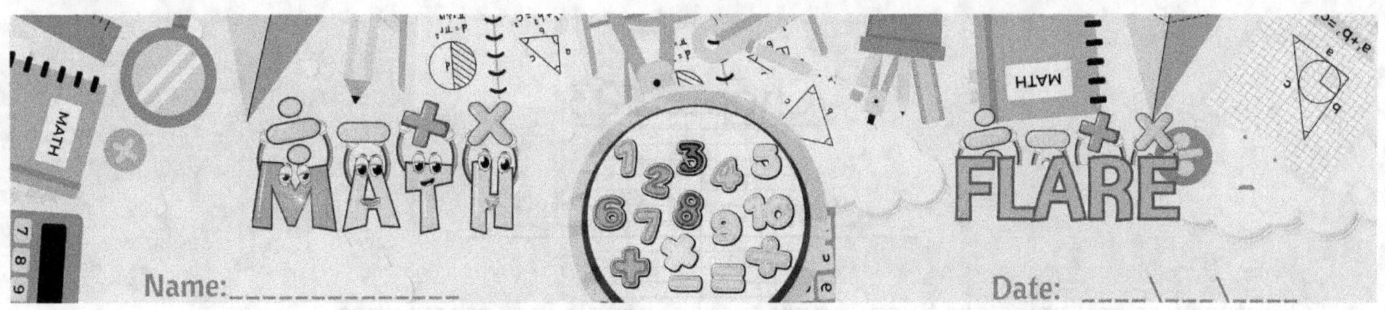

28) Michele made 108 cookies for a bake sale. She put the cookies in bags, with 12 cookies in each bag. How many bags did she have for the bake sale?

29) You have 96 bananas and want to share them equally with two people. How many bananas would each person get?

30) How many 16 cm pieces of rope can you cut from a rope that is 544 cm long?

Chapter. 03

Factors and Multiples

Factors and multiples are two fundamental concepts in mathematics.

Factors

- Factors are numbers that divide another number without leaving a remainder.

- For example, the factors of 12 are 1, 2, 3, 4, 6, and 12 because these numbers can divide 12 evenly.

- Factors always come in pairs, except for perfect squares.

Multiples

- Multiples are the result of multiplying a number by an integer.

- For example, the multiples of 3 are 3, 6, 9, 12, 15, and so on because these numbers are obtained by multiplying 3 by 1, 2, 3, 4, 5, and so on.

- Every number has an infinite number of multiples.

Every factor of a number is a divisor of that number, and every multiple of a number is divisible by that number.

Let's solve some problems:

Factors of 84

2, 3, 4, 6, 7, 12, 14, 21, 28, 42

Multiples of 11

11, 22, 33, 44, 55

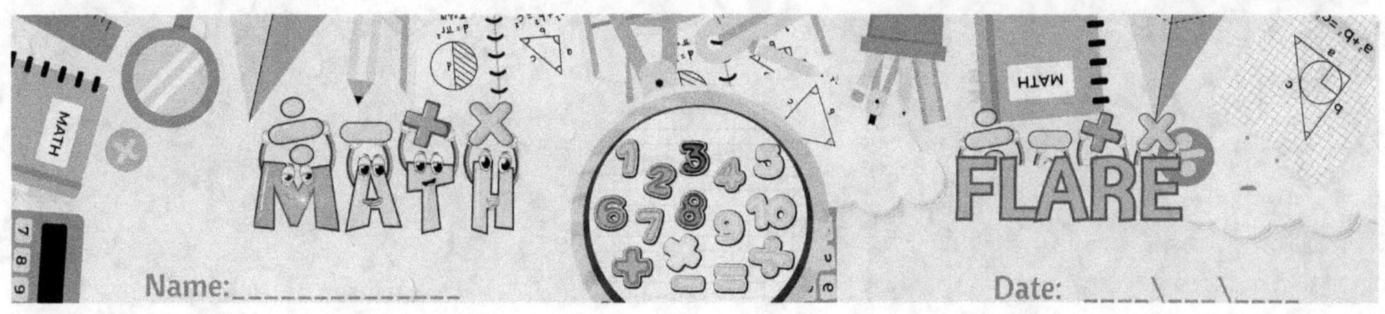

Factors

1) 12   2, 3, 4, 6

2) 84   2, 3, 4, 6, 7, 12, 14, 21, 28, 42

3) 39

4) 70

5) 8

6) 57

7) 97

8) 2 ____

9) 7 ____

10) 4 ____

11) 89 ____

12) 28 ____

13) 1 ____

14) 88 ____

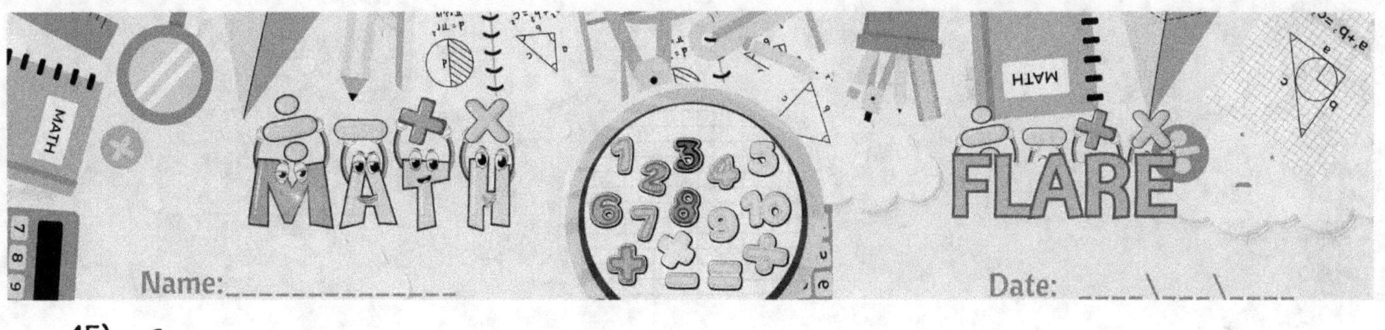

15) 6 _______________________________________

16) 73 _______________________________________

17) 54 _______________________________________

18) 23 _______________________________________

19) 5 _______________________________________

20) 99 _______________________________________

21) 32 _______________________________________

Name:________________ Date: _______________

22) 56 _______________________________________

23) 3 _______________________________________

24) 95 _______________________________________

25) 9 _______________________________________

26) 64 _______________________________________

27) 20 _______________________________________

28) 53 _______________________________________

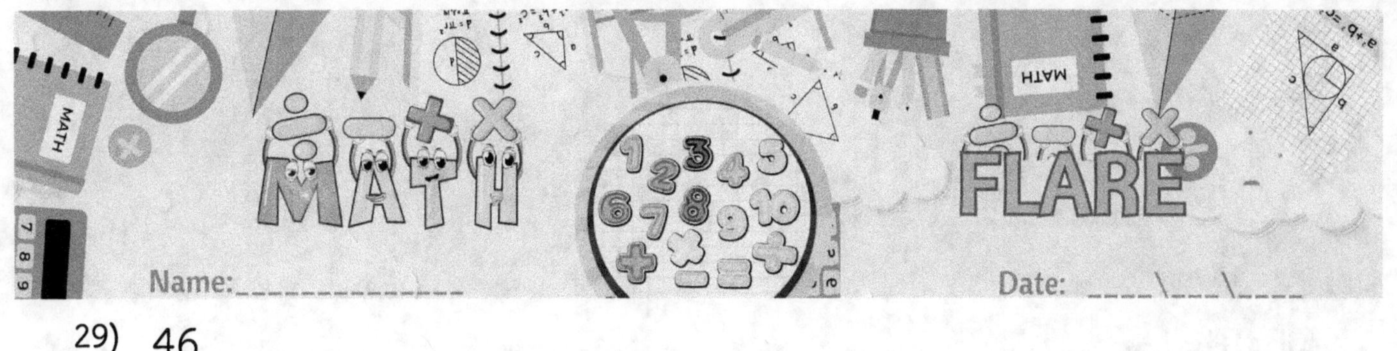

29) 46

30) 40

31) 79

32) 82

33) 47

34) 16

35) 49

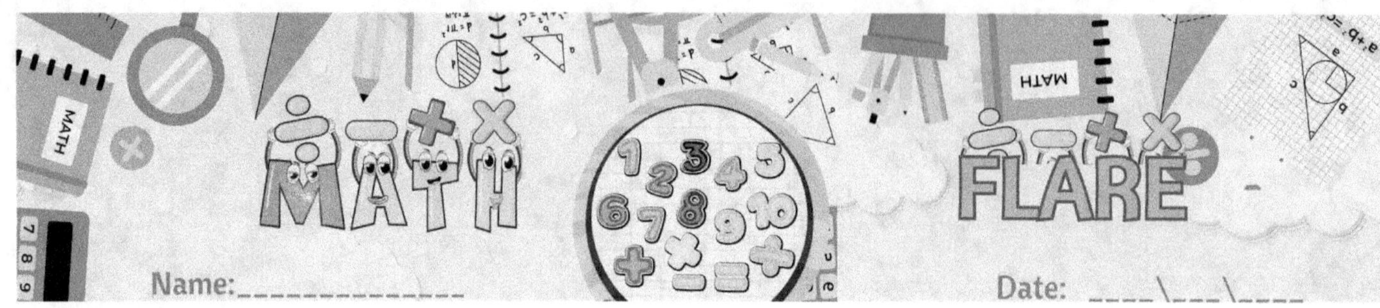

Multiples

List the multiples for each number.

1) 11   11, 22, 33, 44, 55

2) 78

3) 3

4) 84

5) 8

6) 45

7) 73

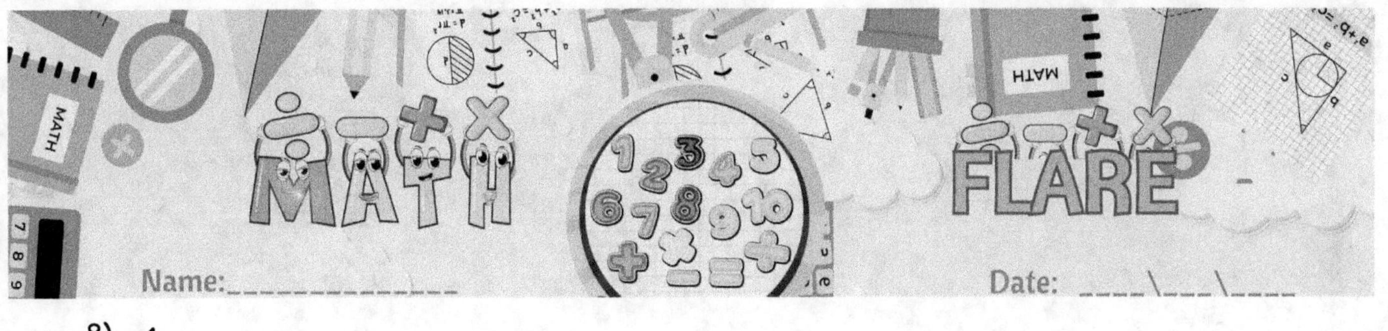

8) 1 ______________________________

9) 42 ______________________________

10) 7 ______________________________

11) 76 ______________________________

12) 23 ______________________________

13) 93 ______________________________

14) 69 ______________________________

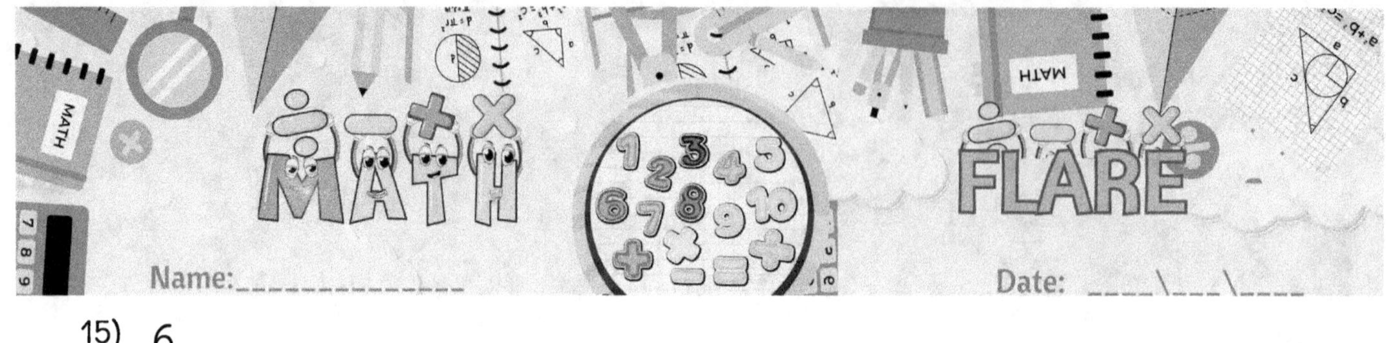

15) 6 _______________________________________

16) 85 _______________________________________

17) 40 _______________________________________

18) 54 _______________________________________

19) 79 _______________________________________

20) 18 _______________________________________

21) 57 _______________________________________

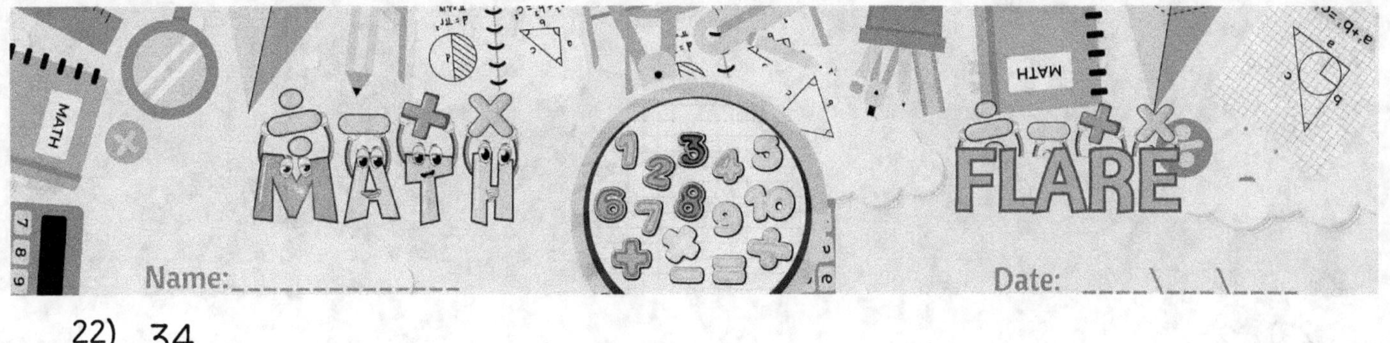

22) 34 ______________________________

23) 92 ______________________________

24) 83 ______________________________

25) 55 ______________________________

26) 4 ______________________________

27) 72 ______________________________

28) 9 ______________________________

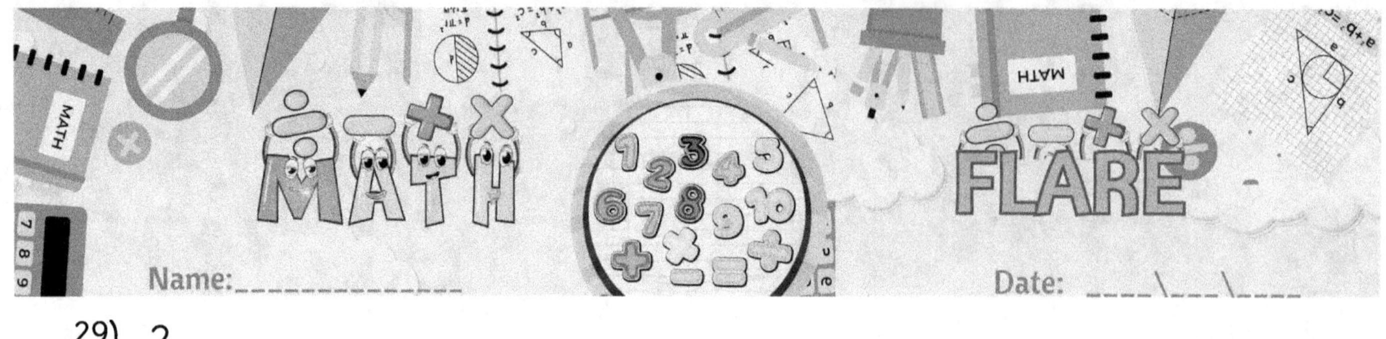

29) 2 _______________________________________

30) 68 _______________________________________

31) 28 _______________________________________

32) 62 _______________________________________

33) 21 _______________________________________

34) 41 _______________________________________

35) 33 _______________________________________

Chapter. 04

Place Value and Expanded Notations

Place value tells us the value of a digit in a number based on where it's placed.

Imagine we have the number 87,647.528. It has 6 digits.

Now, each digit holds a special place. Let's break down the number 87,647.528:

- The digit 8 is in the ten thousands place. Its value is 8×10000=80000.

- The digit 7 is in the thousands place. Its value is 7×1000=7000.

- The digit 6 is in the hundreds place. Its value is 6×100=600.

- The digit 4 is in the tens place. Its value is 4×10=40.

- The digit 7 is in the ones place. Its value is 7×1=7.

- The digit 5 is in the tenths place. Its value is $5 \times \frac{1}{10} = 0.5$.

- The digit 2 is in the hundredths place. Its value is $2 \times \frac{1}{100} = 0.02$.

- The digit 8 is in the thousandths place. Its value is $8 \times \frac{1}{1000} = 0.008$.

When we add these values together, we find the value of the entire number:

$$80000 + 7000 + 600 + 40 + 7 + 0.5 + 0.02 + 0.008 = 87,647.528$$

Let's solve some problems:

Place value of the underlined digit:

$$3{,}7\underline{9}7.455 = \underline{\quad 7 \text{ hundreds} \quad}$$

Expanded notations:

_37,311.07_	30,000 + 7,000 + 300 + 10 + 1 + 0.07
_2,514.153_	2 thousands + 5 hundreds + 1 ten + 4 ones + 1 tenth + 5 hundredths + 3 thousandths
67,039.04	_6 ten thousands + 7 thousands + 3 tens + 9 ones + 4 hundredths_

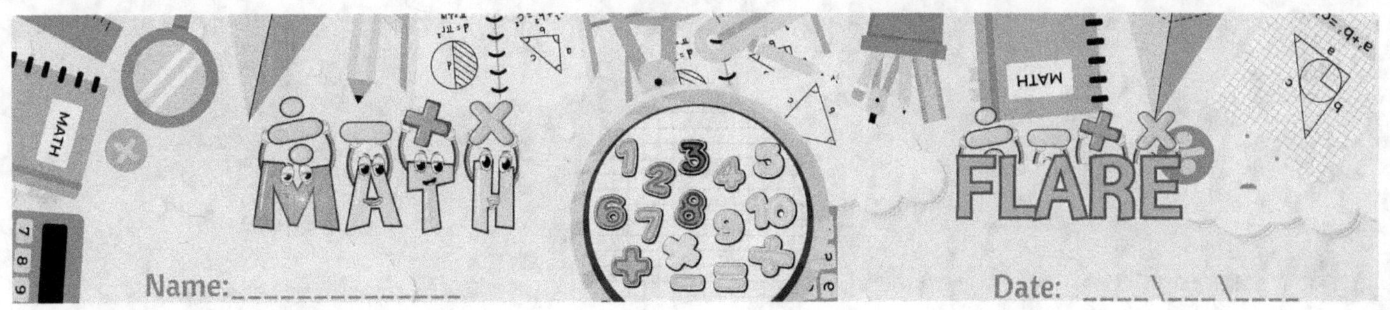

Place Value

Determine the place value of the underlined digit.

1) 3,797.455 = _______ 7 hundreds _______

2) 9,748.907 = _______

3) 6,580,452 = _______

4) 38,078.47 = _______

5) 2,828.555 = _______

6) 6,192.982 = _______

7) 13,174.72 = _______

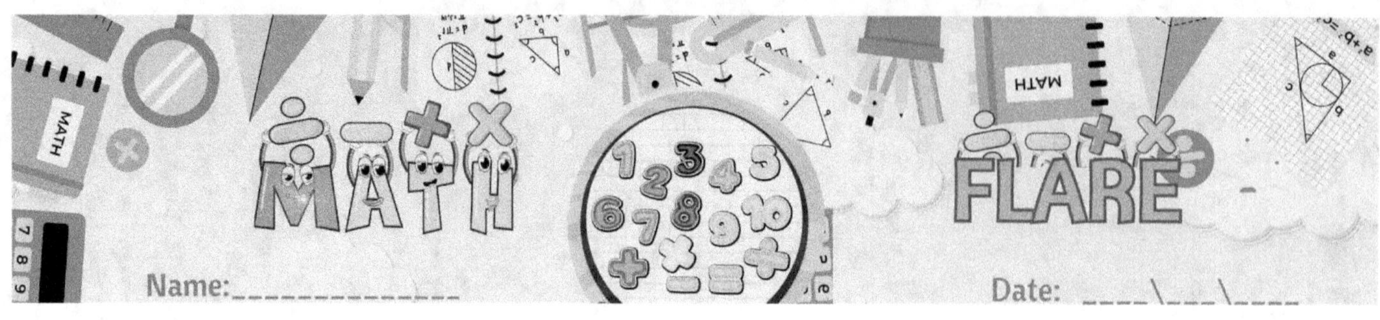

8) 5,2̲67.389 = ________________________________

9) 9,126,1̲58 = ________________________________

10) 4̲,502.668 = ________________________________

11) 2̲9,641.46 = ________________________________

12) 1,65̲8,933 = ________________________________

13) 23,5̲77.85 = ________________________________

14) 33,06̲6.07 = ________________________________

15) 9,785.32̲3 = ________________________________

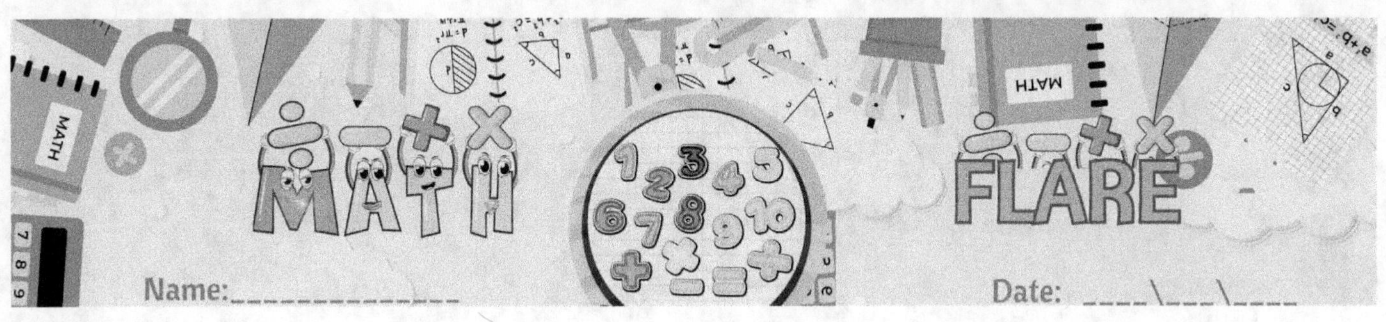

16) 784,245.1 = ______________________

17) 4,501.049 = ______________________

18) 2,971,934 = ______________________

19) 2,735,573 = ______________________

20) 3,408,622 = ______________________

21) 6,349.955 = ______________________

22) 7,222.233 = ______________________

23) 53,899.99 = ______________________

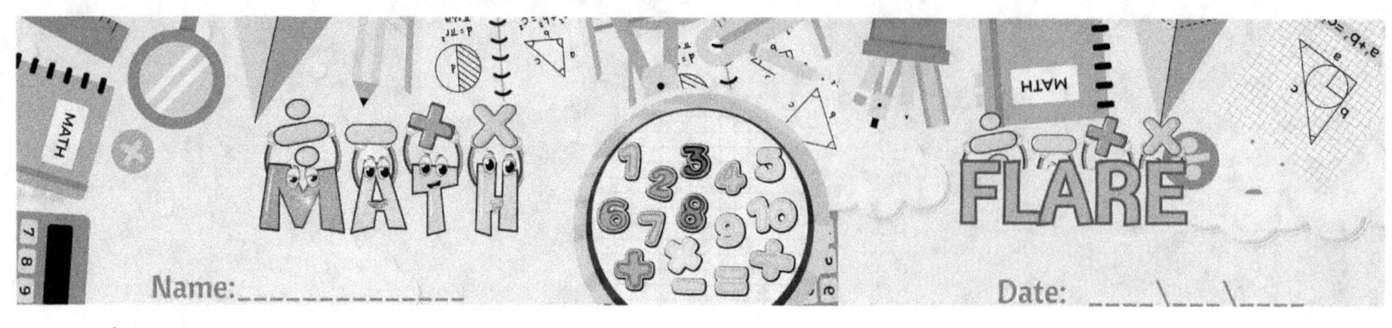

24) 3,216.93<u>5</u> = _______________________

25) 6,25<u>5</u>,399 = _______________________

26) 601,<u>3</u>59.1 = _______________________

27) 69,<u>0</u>27.43 = _______________________

28) 81,67<u>9</u>.01 = _______________________

29) 9,1<u>0</u>0.914 = _______________________

30) <u>2</u>,174,162 = _______________________

31) 4,494,4<u>5</u>4 = _______________________

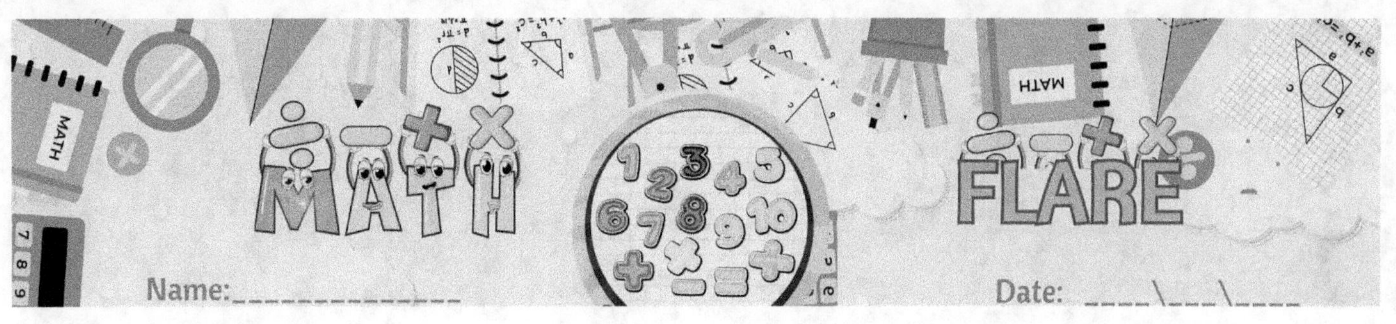

32) $\underline{8}0,417.2$ = _______________________________

33) $49,915.\underline{7}3$ = _______________________________

34) $2,\underline{1}44,337$ = _______________________________

35) $3,46\underline{8}.153$ = _______________________________

36) $793,8\underline{2}9.1$ = _______________________________

37) $6,\underline{2}21.254$ = _______________________________

38) $11\underline{2},024.5$ = _______________________________

39) $84,\underline{4}60.7$ = _______________________________

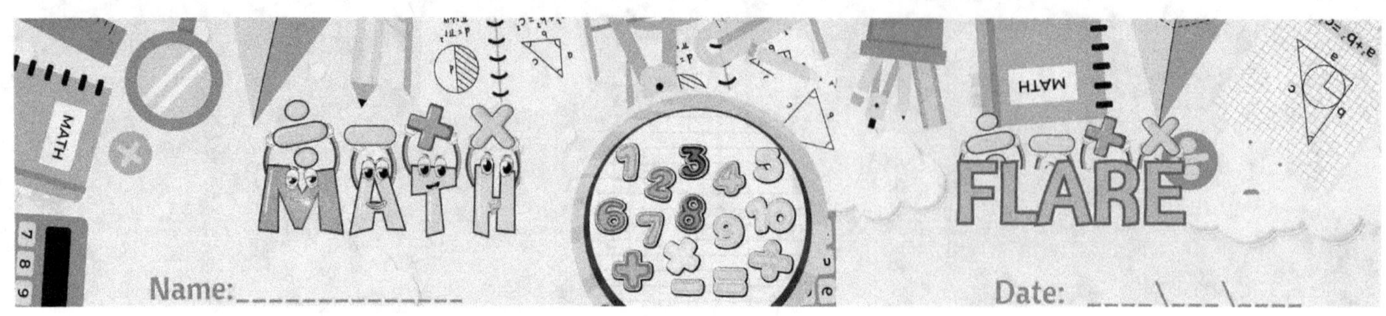

Place Value: Expanded Notation

Provide the expanded notation for each value.

1) _____37,311.07_____ 30,000 + 7,000 + 300 + 10 + 1 + 0.07

2) _______________ 500,000 + 50,000 + 2,000 + 700 + 10 + 3 + 0.5

3) _______________ 5,000 + 900 + 60 + 0.5 + 0.03 + 0.008

4) _______________ 60,000 + 3,000 + 700 + 30 + 1 + 0.5 + 0.01

5) _______________ 800,000 + 10,000 + 7,000 + 300 + 90 + 8 + 0.5

6) _______________ 400,000 + 50,000 + 3,000 + 600 + 30 + 8 + 0.6

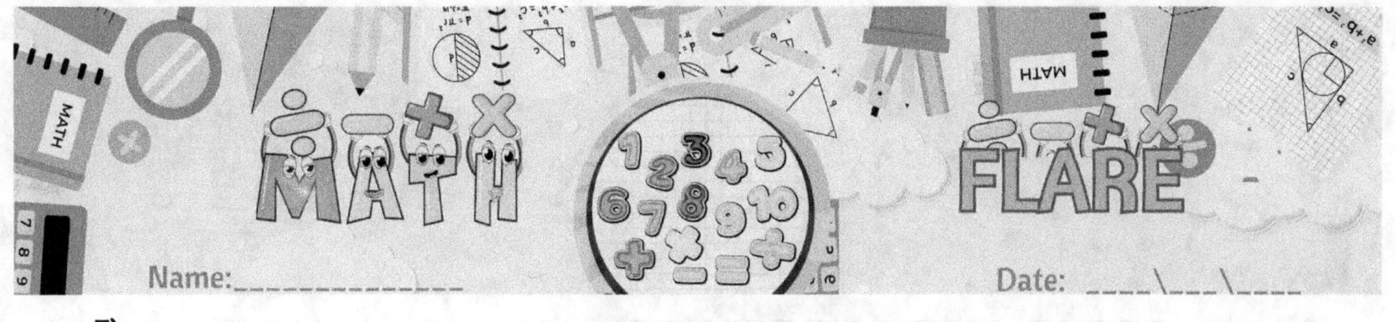

7) ___________________ 4,000,000 + 500,000 + 30,000 + 6,000 + 900 + 40 + 3

8) ___________________ 9,000 + 10 + 7 + 0.4 + 0.02 + 0.005

9) ___________________ 3,000,000 + 300,000 + 40,000 + 8,000 + 900 + 90 + 9

10) ___________________ 50,000 + 7,000 + 400 + 20 + 5 + 0.4 + 0.03

11) ___________________ 900,000 + 30,000 + 400 + 80 + 4 + 0.7

12) ___________________ 6,000,000 + 700,000 + 70,000 + 5,000 + 700 + 10 + 1

13) ___________________ 2,000,000 + 800,000 + 70,000 + 7,000 + 600 + 20 + 4

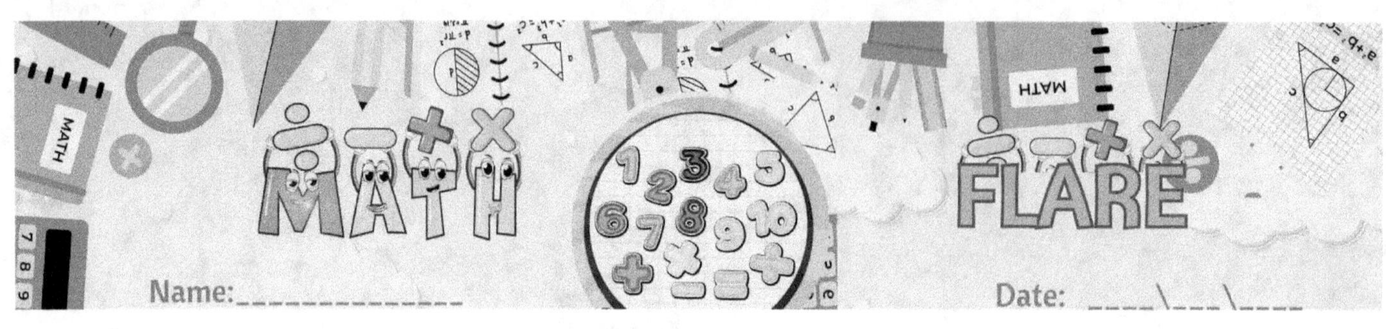

14) _________________________ 3,000,000 + 100,000 + 40,000 + 30 + 6

15) _________________________ 70,000 + 1,000 + 700 + 60 + 0.2 + 0.02

16) _________________________ 200,000 + 70,000 + 5,000 + 100 + 30 + 0.6

17) _________________________ 300,000 + 60,000 + 7,000 + 800 + 10 + 3 + 0.5

18) _________________________ 800,000 + 10,000 + 5,000 + 100 + 10 + 0.9

19) _________________________ 9,000 + 600 + 5 + 0.3 + 0.09 + 0.005

20) _________________________ 2,000,000 + 500,000 + 1,000 + 300 + 50 + 2

21) ________________   1,000,000 + 30,000 + 2,000 + 200 + 40 + 7

22) ________________   50,000 + 5,000 + 700 + 40 + 9 + 0.4 + 0.08

23) ________________   2,000,000 + 500,000 + 70,000 + 1,000 + 200 + 40 + 4

24) ________________   70,000 + 9,000 + 900 + 10 + 6 + 0.04

25) ________________   600,000 + 90,000 + 3,000 + 400 + 30 + 4 + 0.9

26) ________________   2,000 + 900 + 10 + 7 + 0.2 + 0.04 + 0.008

27) ________________   800,000 + 70,000 + 3,000 + 400 + 90 + 6 + 0.7

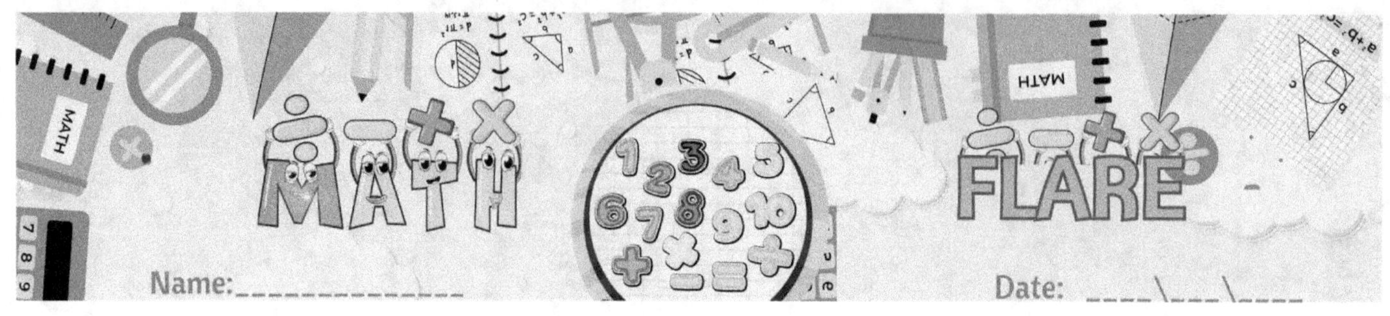

28) _________________________ 400,000 + 50,000 + 8,000 + 300 + 70 + 2 + 0.6

29) _________________________ 6,000,000 + 40,000 + 3,000 + 300 + 50 + 8

30) _________________________ 30,000 + 9,000 + 400 + 50 + 5 + 0.2 + 0.03

31) _________________________ 900,000 + 20,000 + 6,000 + 700 + 60 + 4 + 0.8

32) _________________________ 90,000 + 7,000 + 600 + 30 + 4 + 0.6 + 0.01

33) _________________________ 10,000 + 8,000 + 100 + 30 + 0.08

34) _________________________ 200,000 + 80,000 + 9,000 + 400 + 70 + 5 + 0.6

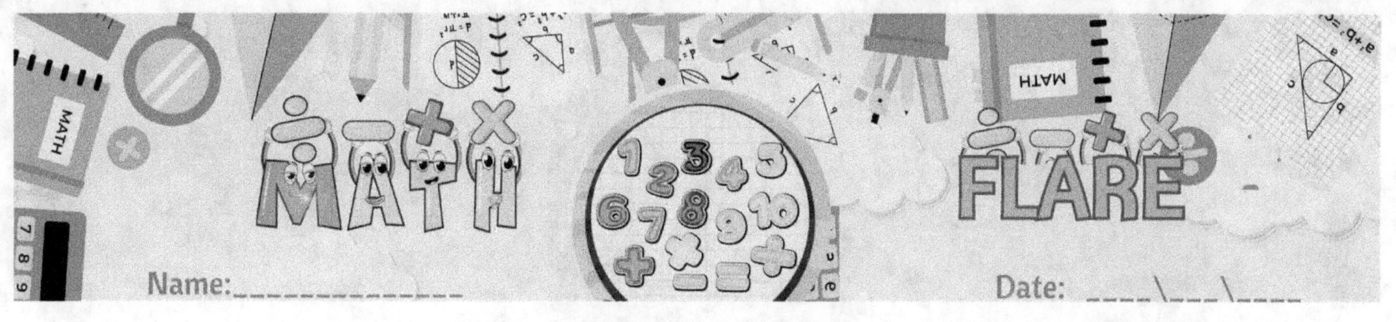

35) _________________ $60,000 + 9,000 + 800 + 30 + 1 + 0.1 + 0.09$

36) _________________ $1,000 + 200 + 4 + 0.7 + 0.08 + 0.002$

37) _________________ $9,000 + 200 + 60 + 2 + 0.4 + 0.002$

38) _________________ $7,000,000 + 500,000 + 20,000 + 3,000 + 900 + 30 + 5$

39) _________________ $9,000,000 + 30,000 + 3,000 + 800 + 10 + 2$

40) _________________ $1,000 + 200 + 20 + 1 + 0.7 + 0.03 + 0.006$

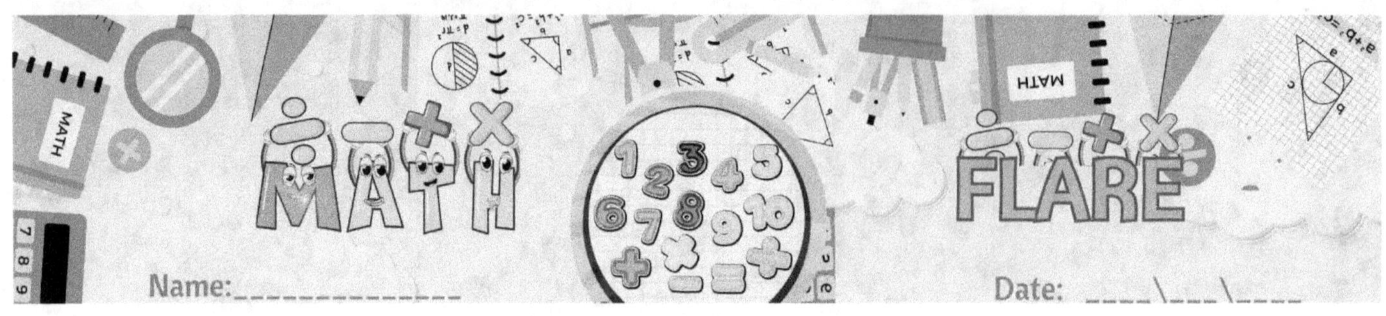

Place Value: Expanded Notation

Provide the expanded notation for each value.

1) _______2,514.153_______ 2 thousands + 5 hundreds + 1 ten + 4 ones + 1 tenth + 5 hundredths + 3 thousandths

2) ___________________ 7 hundred thousands + 7 ten thousands + 6 thousands + 5 hundreds + 2 tens + 9 ones

3) ___________________ 2 ten thousands + 3 thousands + 6 hundreds + 6 tens + 2 ones + 9 tenths + 1 hundredth

4) ___________________ 5 thousands + 8 hundreds + 3 tens + 5 ones + 7 tenths + 8 hundredths + 2 thousandths

5) ___________________ 8 ten thousands + 8 thousands + 7 hundreds + 2 tenths + 1 hundredth

Name:_________________________   Date: ______________

6) ___________________________ 5 thousands + 2 hundreds + 4 tens + 1 one + 9 tenths + 3 hundredths + 5 thousandths

7) ___________________________ 6 ten thousands + 2 thousands + 1 hundred + 3 tens + 3 ones + 4 tenths + 2 hundredths

8) ___________________________ 4 thousands + 4 tens + 7 ones + 4 tenths + 2 hundredths + 2 thousandths

9) ___________________________ 5 hundred thousands + 9 ten thousands + 7 hundreds + 6 tens + 1 one

10) ___________________________ 3 millions + 4 hundred thousands + 1 ten thousand + 8 thousands + 7 hundreds + 8 tens + 3 ones

11) ______________________ 4 ten thousands + 2 thousands + 1 hundred + 4 tens + 7 ones + 9 tenths + 6 hundredths

12) ______________________ 5 ten thousands + 4 thousands + 2 hundreds + 8 tens + 2 ones + 7 tenths + 3 hundredths

13) ______________________ 3 millions + 2 hundred thousands + 5 ten thousands + 2 thousands + 3 hundreds + 4 tens

14) ______________________ 2 millions + 6 ten thousands + 6 thousands + 4 hundreds + 4 tens + 4 ones

15) ______________________ 2 thousands + 5 hundreds + 9 tens + 8 ones + 8 tenths + 6 hundredths

16) _______________________ 8 hundred thousands + 1 ten thousand + 5 thousands + 6 hundreds + 1 ten + 5 ones + 8 tenths

17) _______________________ 3 thousands + 9 hundreds + 5 tens + 5 ones + 8 tenths + 9 hundredths + 1 thousandth

18) _______________________ 7 hundred thousands + 9 ten thousands + 6 thousands + 8 hundreds + 9 tens + 3 ones + 3 tenths

19) _______________________ 9 ten thousands + 4 thousands + 3 hundreds + 8 tens + 8 ones + 1 hundredth

20) _______________________ 6 hundred thousands + 2 ten thousands + 5 thousands + 6 hundreds + 7 tens + 3 ones + 8 tenths

21) _________________________ 5 ten thousands + 8 thousands + 1 ten + 4 ones + 1 tenth + 8 hundredths

22) _________________________ 9 ten thousands + 9 thousands + 5 hundreds + 3 tens + 2 ones + 1 tenth + 6 hundredths

23) _________________________ 3 hundred thousands + 9 ten thousands + 7 thousands + 4 hundreds + 6 ones + 8 tenths

24) _________________________ 9 millions + 4 hundred thousands + 3 thousands + 4 hundreds + 7 tens + 5 ones

25) _________________________ 6 ten thousands + 4 thousands + 7 hundreds + 4 tens + 8 ones + 9 tenths + 3 hundredths

26) _______________________   9 hundred thousands + 5 ten thousands + 4 thousands + 1 hundred + 3 tens + 8 ones + 5 tenths

27) _______________________   5 thousands + 9 hundreds + 6 tens + 2 ones + 7 tenths + 3 thousandths

28) _______________________   9 ten thousands + 9 thousands + 8 hundreds + 2 tens + 8 ones + 6 tenths + 7 hundredths

29) _______________________   6 ten thousands + 1 thousand + 5 hundreds + 6 tens + 9 ones + 1 tenth + 5 hundredths

30) _______________________   6 ten thousands + 9 thousands + 7 hundreds + 1 ten + 2 ones + 4 tenths + 1 hundredth

31) _________________________ 3 millions + 4 hundred thousands + 8 ten thousands + 8 thousands + 9 hundreds + 3 ones

32) _________________________ 6 millions + 1 hundred thousand + 5 ten thousands + 4 thousands + 1 hundred + 9 tens + 9 ones

33) _________________________ 9 thousands + 1 hundred + 1 ten + 7 ones + 2 tenths + 9 hundredths + 6 thousandths

34) _________________________ 9 hundred thousands + 3 ten thousands + 8 thousands + 3 hundreds + 6 tens + 5 ones + 9 tenths

35) _________________________ 9 thousands + 9 hundreds + 8 tens + 7 ones + 1 tenth + 9 hundredths + 8 thousandths

36) _______________________ 3 millions + 2 hundred thousands + 6 ten thousands + 6 thousands + 9 hundreds + 5 tens + 6 ones

37) _______________________ 4 ten thousands + 2 thousands + 8 tens + 6 ones + 5 tenths + 7 hundredths

38) _______________________ 6 hundred thousands + 7 ten thousands + 3 thousands + 5 hundreds + 4 tens + 6 ones + 1 tenth

39) _______________________ 9 millions + 1 hundred thousand + 2 ten thousands + 1 thousand + 5 hundreds + 8 tens + 2 ones

40) _______________________ 2 hundred thousands + 6 ten thousands + 9 thousands + 2 hundreds + 4 tens + 1 one + 4 tenths

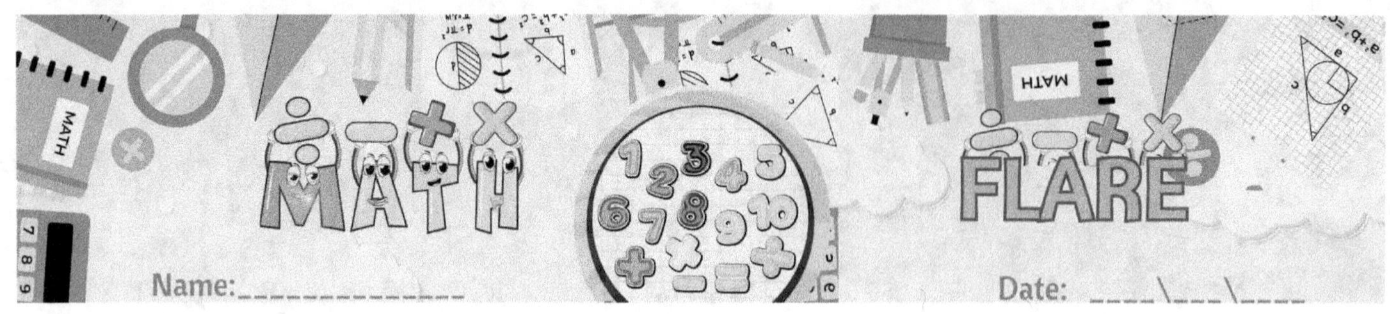

Place Value: Expanded Notation

Provide the expanded notation for each value.

1) 67,039.04   6 ten thousands + 7 thousands + 3 tens + 9 ones + 4 hundredths

2) 5,687,546

3) 8,676.116

4) 36,245.75

5) 9,730.726

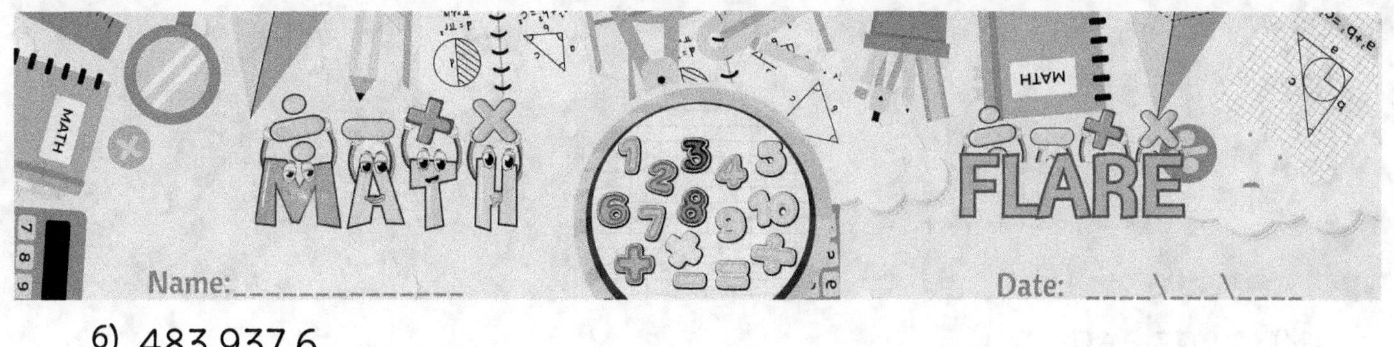

6) 483,937.6 _______________________________

____

7) 7,511,121 _______________________________

____

8) 9,746,563 _______________________________

____

9) 1,295,896 _______________________________

____

10) 8,826.961 _______________________________

____

11) 72,488.90 _______________________________

____

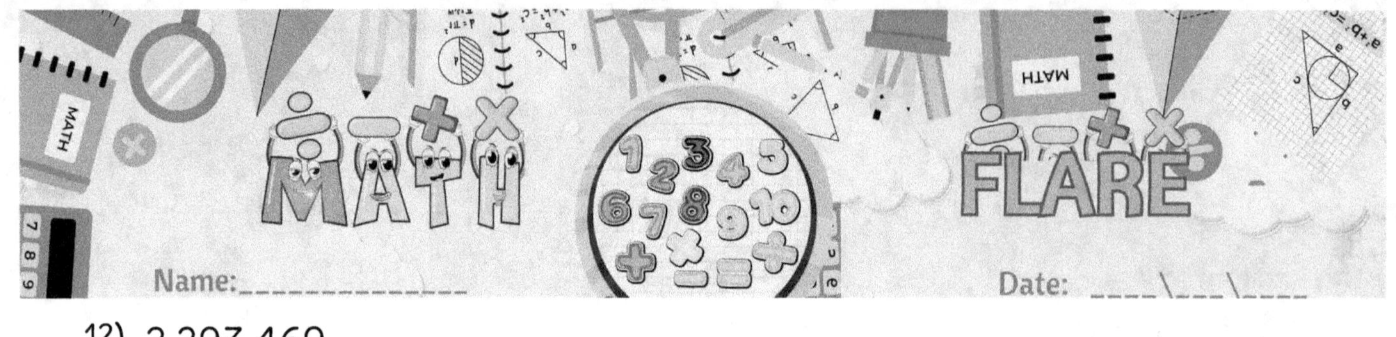

12) 2,293,469 ______________________

13) 8,085,133 ______________________

14) 377,707.4 ______________________

15) 54,203.17 ______________________

16) 25,609.36 ______________________

17) 47,912.22 ______________________

18) 2,962,815 _______________________________

____

19) 9,360,888 _______________________________

____

20) 932,863.5 _______________________________

____

21) 9,279.231 _______________________________

____

22) 6,230,474 _______________________________

____

23) 7,890,505 _______________________________

____

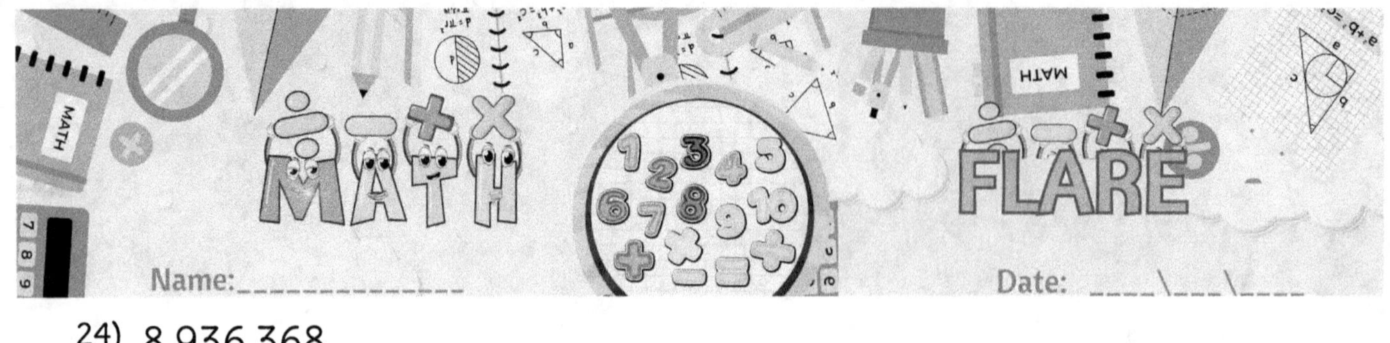

24) 8,936,368 _______________________________

25) 99,298.79 _______________________________

26) 80,605.95 _______________________________

27) 6,310,976 _______________________________

28) 3,868.680 _______________________________

29) 20,792.45 _______________________________

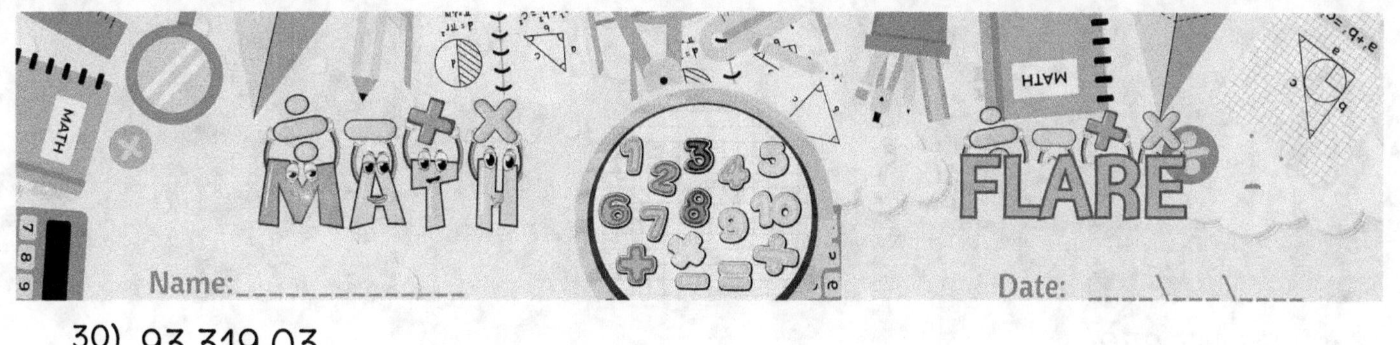

30) 93,319.03 _______________________________

____

31) 4,947,501 _______________________________

____

32) 72,204.29 _______________________________

____

33) 884,735.0 _______________________________

____

34) 7,746,386 _______________________________

____

35) 9,552.832 _______________________________

____

36) 1,113,872 _______________________________

37) 2,277.100 _______________________________

38) 134,949.3 _______________________________

39) 96,727.48 _______________________________

40) 2,635,518 _______________________________

41) 303,026.4 _______________________________

Chapter. 05

Fractions

Fractions represent parts of a whole. They consist of a numerator (the number on top) and a denominator (the number on the bottom).

For example: we have an orange, and we divide it into 5 equal slices. Each slice represents $\frac{1}{5}$ of the orange. Now, if we take 3 of those slices, we have taken $\frac{3}{5}$ of the orange.

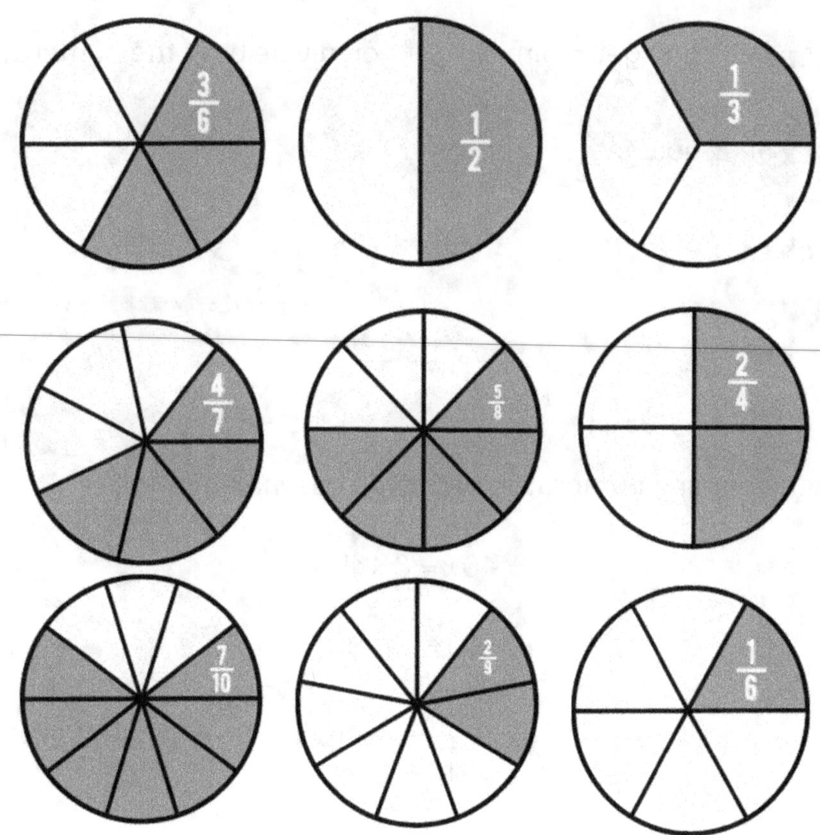

<u>Equivalent Fractions</u>

Equivalent fractions are fractions that represent the same value or part of a whole, even though they may look different.

To find equivalent fractions, you can:

- Multiply or divide both the numerator and denominator by the same nonzero number.
- Simplify fractions to their simplest form.

$\frac{1}{2}$ and $\frac{2}{4}$ are equivalent fractions because if you multiply the numerator and denominator of $\frac{1}{2}$ by 2, you get $\frac{2}{4}$. Similarly, if you divide both the numerator and denominator of $\frac{2}{4}$ by 2, you get $\frac{1}{2}$.

Let's solve a problem:

$$\frac{}{8} = \frac{15}{40}$$

To solve the missing numerator, we can cross multiply.

$$40x = 8 \times 15$$

$$40x = 120$$

$$x = \frac{120}{40} = x = 3$$

$$\frac{3}{8} = \frac{15}{40}$$

Fractions Addition (Common Denominator)

To add fractions with a common denominator, we add their numerators together and keep the denominator the same.

For example: if we want to add $\frac{3}{5}$ and $\frac{2}{5}$ both fractions have the same denominator of 5.

Therefore, to add them, we simply add their numerators:

$$\frac{3}{5} + \frac{2}{5} = \frac{3+2}{5} = \frac{5}{5}$$

Let's solve a problem:

$$\frac{9}{17} + \frac{1}{17} = \frac{9+1}{17} = \frac{10}{17}$$

Fractions Subtraction (Common Denominator)

To subtract fractions with a common denominator, we find the difference between their numerators and keep the denominator the same.

For example:

$$\frac{3}{5} - \frac{2}{5} = \frac{3-2}{5} = \frac{1}{5}$$

Let's solve a problem:

$$\frac{15}{16} - \frac{12}{16} = \frac{15-12}{16} = \frac{3}{16}$$

Fractions Multiplication

To multiply fractions, we simply multiply the numerators together to get the new numerator and multiply the denominators together to get the new denominator.

For example, let's multiply: $\dfrac{2}{4} \times \dfrac{1}{4}$

Numerator: 2 × 1 = 2

Denominator: 4 × 4 = 16

Therefore, $\dfrac{2}{16}$

we can simplify the resulting fraction:

$$\dfrac{1}{8}$$

Let's solve a problem:

$$\dfrac{4}{5} \times \dfrac{4}{5} = \dfrac{4 \times 4}{5 \times 5} = \dfrac{16}{25}$$

Fractions Division

To divide fractions, we multiply by the reciprocal of the divisor.

For example, let's divide:

$$\dfrac{6}{8} \div \dfrac{4}{8}$$

$$\dfrac{6}{8} \times \dfrac{8}{4} = \dfrac{48}{32} = \dfrac{3}{2}$$

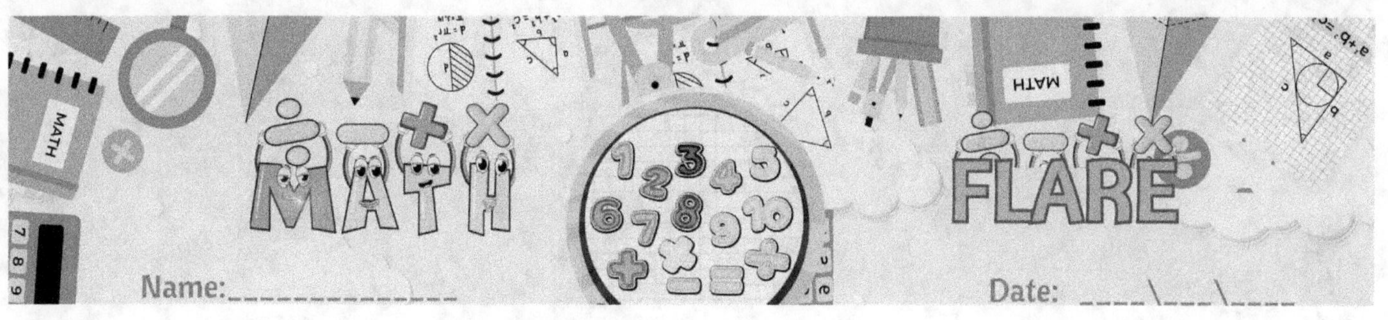

Equivalent Fractions

1) $\dfrac{3}{8} = \dfrac{15}{40}$

2) $\dfrac{7}{12} = \dfrac{21}{}$

3) $\dfrac{}{9} = \dfrac{4}{18}$

4) $\dfrac{}{11} = \dfrac{90}{99}$

5) $\dfrac{1}{} = \dfrac{9}{18}$

6) $\dfrac{}{7} = \dfrac{3}{21}$

7) $\dfrac{}{5} = \dfrac{4}{10}$

8) $\dfrac{3}{4} = \dfrac{}{20}$

9) $\dfrac{}{10} = \dfrac{25}{50}$

10) $\dfrac{3}{6} = \dfrac{18}{}$

11) $\dfrac{1}{3} = \dfrac{}{27}$

12) $\dfrac{2}{} = \dfrac{10}{45}$

13) $\dfrac{6}{12} = \dfrac{}{60}$

14) $\dfrac{1}{4} = \dfrac{2}{}$

15) $\dfrac{1}{2} = \dfrac{}{10}$

16) $\dfrac{2}{10} = \dfrac{}{100}$

17) $\dfrac{4}{11} = \dfrac{}{110}$

18) $\dfrac{1}{} = \dfrac{9}{45}$

19) $\dfrac{2}{} = \dfrac{10}{15}$

20) $\dfrac{5}{8} = \dfrac{}{32}$

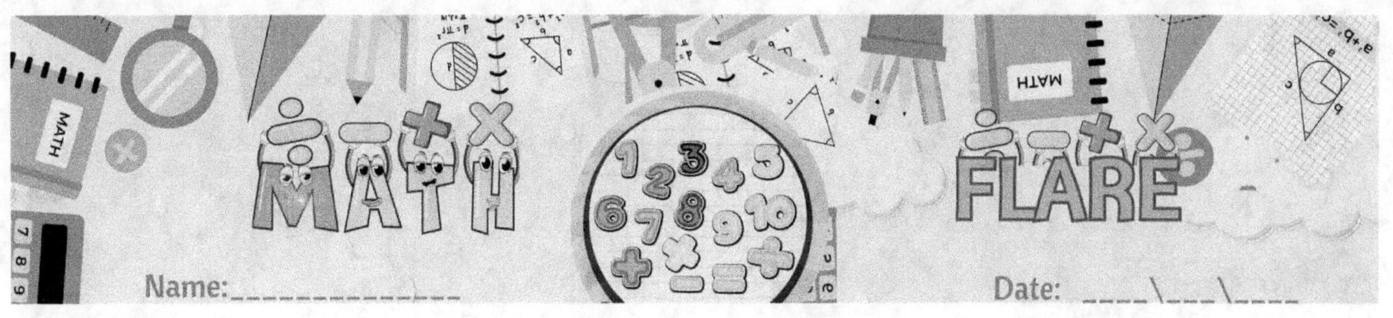

Name:_________________ Date: _______________

21) $\dfrac{1}{6} = \dfrac{7}{}$

22) $\dfrac{2}{7} = \dfrac{}{70}$

23) $\dfrac{2}{3} = \dfrac{16}{}$

24) $\dfrac{2}{7} = \dfrac{10}{}$

25) $\dfrac{1}{2} = \dfrac{}{6}$

26) $\dfrac{}{6} = \dfrac{5}{30}$

27) $\dfrac{2}{4} = \dfrac{14}{}$

28) $\dfrac{4}{} = \dfrac{8}{18}$

29) $\dfrac{}{10} = \dfrac{35}{50}$

30) $\dfrac{3}{5} = \dfrac{30}{}$

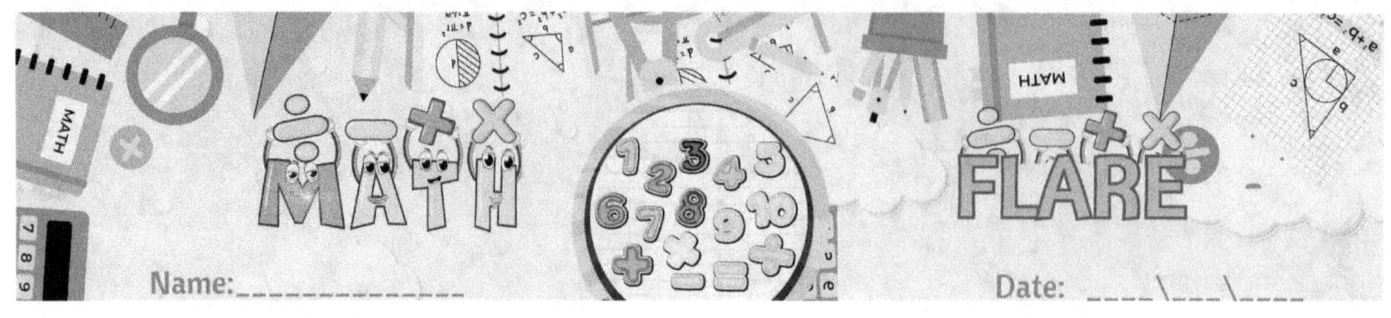

Fractions Addition (Common Denominator)

Find the sum.

1) $\frac{9}{17} + \frac{1}{17} =$ $\frac{9+1}{17} = \frac{10}{17}$

2) $\frac{8}{20} + \frac{8}{20} =$ _______________

3) $\frac{4}{13} + \frac{4}{13} =$ _______________

4) $\frac{5}{16} + \frac{3}{16} =$ _______________

5) $\frac{2}{11} + \frac{8}{11} =$ _______________

6) $\frac{1}{4} + \frac{1}{4} =$ _______________

7) $\frac{4}{7} + \frac{2}{7} =$ _______________

8) $\frac{1}{19} + \frac{9}{19} =$ _______________

9) $\frac{1}{20} + \frac{5}{20} =$ _______________

10) $\frac{2}{12} + \frac{3}{12} =$ _______________

11) $\frac{10}{13} + \frac{1}{13} =$ _______________

12) $\frac{2}{6} + \frac{1}{6} =$ _______________

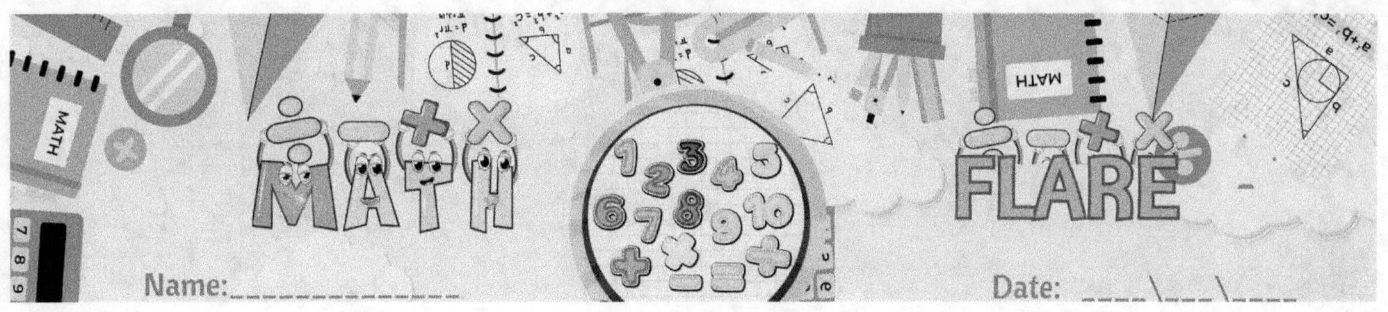

13) $\dfrac{4}{16} + \dfrac{1}{16} =$ _______________

14) $\dfrac{1}{5} + \dfrac{2}{5} =$ _______________

15) $\dfrac{9}{11} + \dfrac{1}{11} =$ _______________

16) $\dfrac{1}{2} + \dfrac{1}{2} =$ _______________

17) $\dfrac{1}{8} + \dfrac{4}{8} =$ _______________

18) $\dfrac{4}{15} + \dfrac{6}{15} =$ _______________

19) $\dfrac{7}{10} + \dfrac{1}{10} =$ _______________

20) $\dfrac{2}{14} + \dfrac{7}{14} =$ _______________

21) $\dfrac{2}{4} + \dfrac{1}{4} =$ _______________

22) $\dfrac{1}{18} + \dfrac{1}{18} =$ _______________

23) $\dfrac{1}{9} + \dfrac{7}{9} =$ _______________

24) $\dfrac{1}{3} + \dfrac{1}{3} =$ _______________

25) $\dfrac{4}{8} + \dfrac{1}{8} =$ _______________

26) $\dfrac{2}{18} + \dfrac{1}{18} =$ _______________

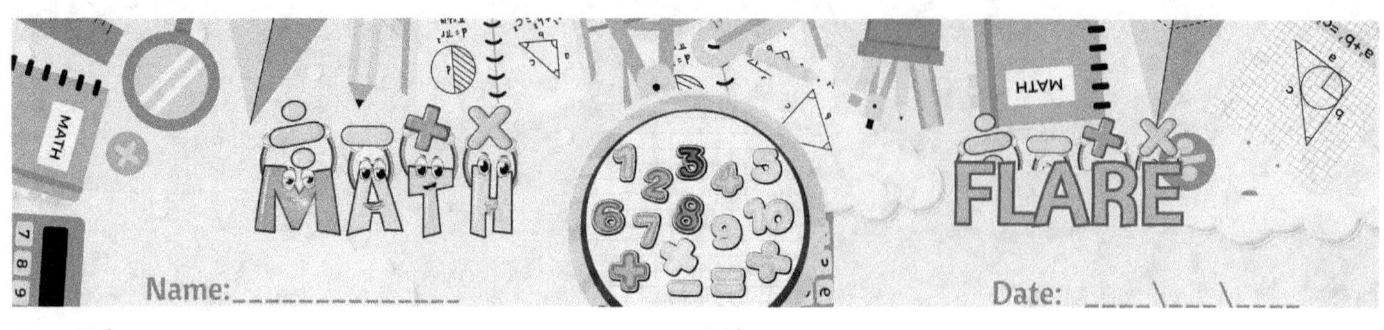

27) $\dfrac{3}{5} + \dfrac{1}{5} =$ _______________

28) $\dfrac{8}{14} + \dfrac{3}{14} =$ _______________

29) $\dfrac{14}{20} + \dfrac{4}{20} =$ _______________

30) $\dfrac{9}{16} + \dfrac{6}{16} =$ _______________

31) $\dfrac{1}{9} + \dfrac{6}{9} =$ _______________

32) $\dfrac{7}{13} + \dfrac{4}{13} =$ _______________

33) $\dfrac{1}{11} + \dfrac{1}{11} =$ _______________

34) $\dfrac{4}{19} + \dfrac{4}{19} =$ _______________

35) $\dfrac{2}{10} + \dfrac{4}{10} =$ _______________

36) $\dfrac{5}{17} + \dfrac{2}{17} =$ _______________

37) $\dfrac{2}{7} + \dfrac{3}{7} =$ _______________

38) $\dfrac{2}{15} + \dfrac{10}{15} =$ _______________

39) $\dfrac{1}{6} + \dfrac{3}{6} =$ _______________

40) $\dfrac{6}{12} + \dfrac{4}{12} =$ _______________

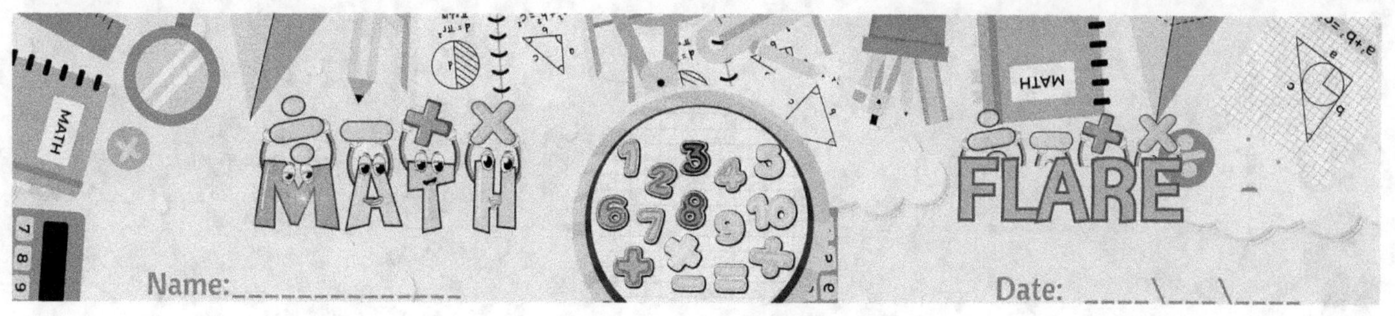

41) $\dfrac{9}{19} + \dfrac{5}{19} =$ _______________

42) $\dfrac{5}{12} + \dfrac{6}{12} =$ _______________

43) $\dfrac{4}{16} + \dfrac{11}{16} =$ _______________

44) $\dfrac{1}{6} + \dfrac{1}{6} =$ _______________

45) $\dfrac{1}{8} + \dfrac{1}{8} =$ _______________

46) $\dfrac{6}{13} + \dfrac{5}{13} =$ _______________

47) $\dfrac{12}{18} + \dfrac{4}{18} =$ _______________

48) $\dfrac{3}{7} + \dfrac{2}{7} =$ _______________

49) $\dfrac{6}{17} + \dfrac{1}{17} =$ _______________

50) $\dfrac{1}{15} + \dfrac{3}{15} =$ _______________

51) $\dfrac{7}{20} + \dfrac{4}{20} =$ _______________

52) $\dfrac{2}{9} + \dfrac{5}{9} =$ _______________

53) $\dfrac{2}{11} + \dfrac{3}{11} =$ _______________

54) $\dfrac{4}{10} + \dfrac{3}{10} =$ _______________

55) $\dfrac{2}{5} + \dfrac{2}{5} =$ _______________

56) $\dfrac{3}{14} + \dfrac{4}{14} =$ _______________

57) $\dfrac{9}{14} + \dfrac{2}{14} =$ _______________

58) $\dfrac{7}{18} + \dfrac{3}{18} =$ _______________

59) $\dfrac{1}{20} + \dfrac{16}{20} =$ _______________

60) $\dfrac{2}{13} + \dfrac{9}{13} =$ _______________

61) $\dfrac{5}{12} + \dfrac{1}{12} =$ _______________

62) $\dfrac{2}{9} + \dfrac{1}{9} =$ _______________

63) $\dfrac{2}{5} + \dfrac{1}{5} =$ _______________

64) $\dfrac{2}{16} + \dfrac{8}{16} =$ _______________

65) $\dfrac{9}{19} + \dfrac{1}{19} =$ _______________

66) $\dfrac{2}{15} + \dfrac{7}{15} =$ _______________

67) $\dfrac{1}{10} + \dfrac{6}{10} =$ _______________

68) $\dfrac{8}{17} + \dfrac{1}{17} =$ _______________

Name:_________________________   Date: _______________

69) $\dfrac{3}{7} + \dfrac{1}{7} =$ _________________

70) $\dfrac{2}{17} + \dfrac{9}{17} =$ _________________

71) $\dfrac{5}{20} + \dfrac{12}{20} =$ _________________

72) $\dfrac{2}{7} + \dfrac{4}{7} =$ _________________

73) $\dfrac{3}{8} + \dfrac{1}{8} =$ _________________

74) $\dfrac{1}{4} + \dfrac{2}{4} =$ _________________

75) $\dfrac{5}{18} + \dfrac{10}{18} =$ _________________

76) $\dfrac{3}{15} + \dfrac{6}{15} =$ _________________

77) $\dfrac{1}{19} + \dfrac{7}{19} =$ _________________

78) $\dfrac{6}{9} + \dfrac{1}{9} =$ _________________

79) $\dfrac{3}{16} + \dfrac{5}{16} =$ _________________

80) $\dfrac{2}{6} + \dfrac{2}{6} =$ _________________

81) $\dfrac{2}{11} + \dfrac{7}{11} =$ _________________

82) $\dfrac{6}{14} + \dfrac{1}{14} =$ _________________

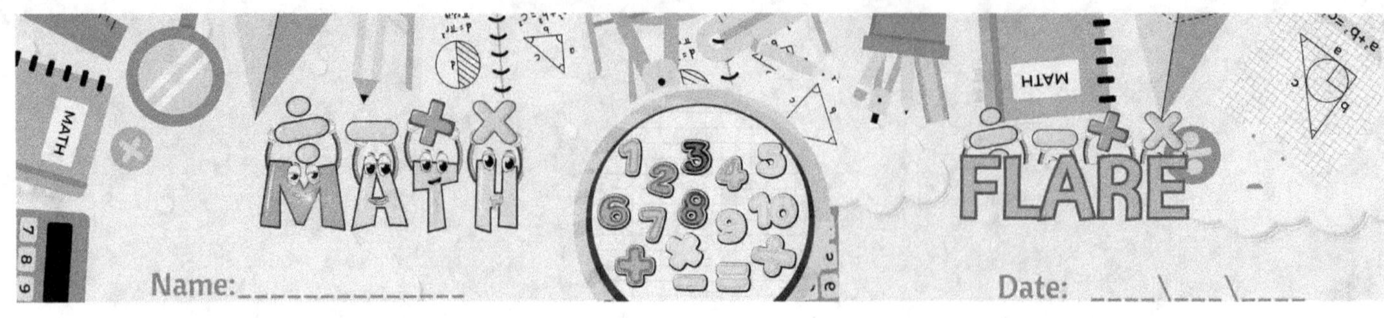

Fractions Subtraction: (Common Denominator)

Find the difference.

1) $\dfrac{15}{16} - \dfrac{12}{16} =$ $\dfrac{15-12}{16} = \dfrac{3}{16}$

2) $\dfrac{15}{17} - \dfrac{12}{17} =$ _______________

3) $\dfrac{12}{14} - \dfrac{11}{14} =$ _______________

4) $\dfrac{2}{4} - \dfrac{1}{4} =$ _______________

5) $\dfrac{3}{5} - \dfrac{1}{5} =$ _______________

6) $\dfrac{2}{3} - \dfrac{1}{3} =$ _______________

7) $\dfrac{18}{20} - \dfrac{14}{20} =$ _______________

8) $\dfrac{5}{10} - \dfrac{3}{10} =$ _______________

9) $\dfrac{16}{17} - \dfrac{14}{17} =$ _______________

10) $\dfrac{5}{9} - \dfrac{4}{9} =$ _______________

11) $\dfrac{11}{12} - \dfrac{10}{12} =$ _______________

12) $\dfrac{11}{15} - \dfrac{1}{15} =$ _______________

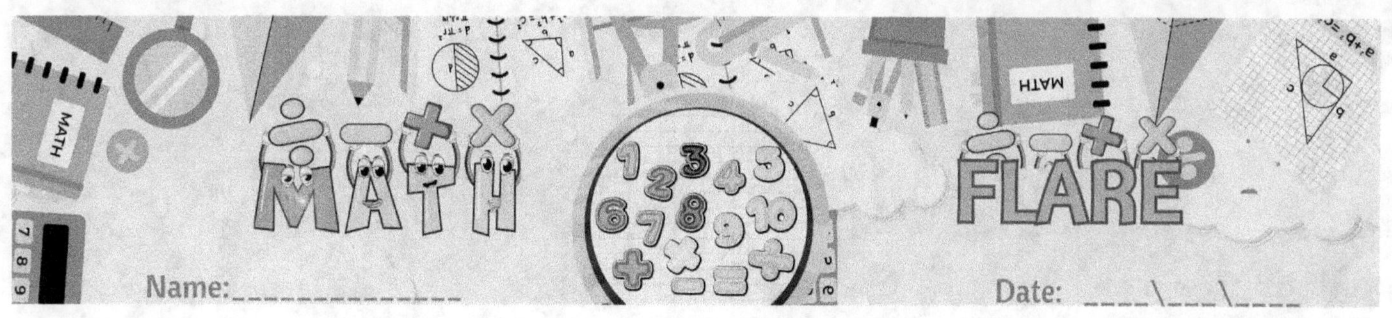

13) $\dfrac{16}{17} - \dfrac{5}{17} =$ _______________

14) $\dfrac{7}{16} - \dfrac{4}{16} =$ _______________

15) $\dfrac{11}{13} - \dfrac{10}{13} =$ _______________

16) $\dfrac{8}{9} - \dfrac{7}{9} =$ _______________

17) $\dfrac{7}{10} - \dfrac{3}{10} =$ _______________

18) $\dfrac{13}{15} - \dfrac{6}{15} =$ _______________

19) $\dfrac{8}{11} - \dfrac{2}{11} =$ _______________

20) $\dfrac{5}{8} - \dfrac{4}{8} =$ _______________

21) $\dfrac{11}{19} - \dfrac{1}{19} =$ _______________

22) $\dfrac{3}{5} - \dfrac{2}{5} =$ _______________

23) $\dfrac{11}{18} - \dfrac{4}{18} =$ _______________

24) $\dfrac{5}{7} - \dfrac{4}{7} =$ _______________

25) $\dfrac{5}{14} - \dfrac{3}{14} =$ _______________

26) $\dfrac{18}{20} - \dfrac{17}{20} =$ _______________

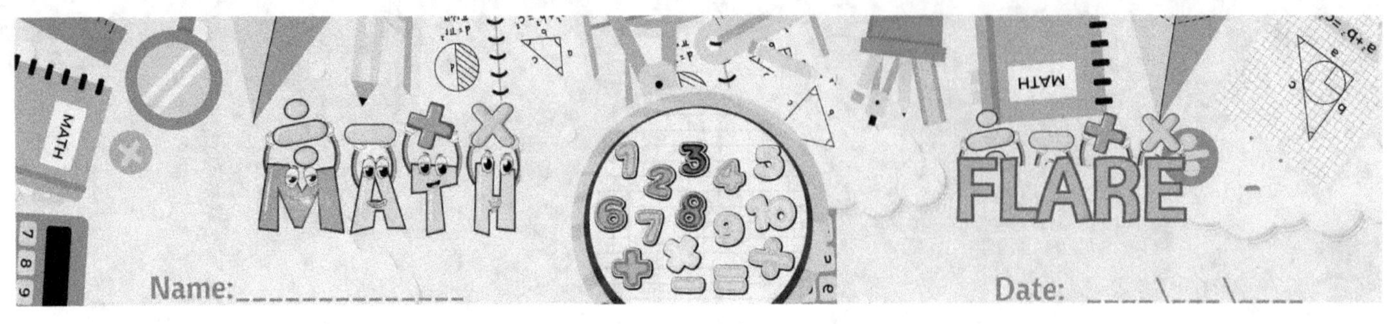

27) $\frac{5}{6} - \frac{2}{6} =$ _________________

28) $\frac{15}{16} - \frac{13}{16} =$ _________________

29) $\frac{10}{14} - \frac{2}{14} =$ _________________

30) $\frac{13}{17} - \frac{12}{17} =$ _________________

31) $\frac{13}{18} - \frac{12}{18} =$ _________________

32) $\frac{9}{12} - \frac{5}{12} =$ _________________

33) $\frac{13}{19} - \frac{9}{19} =$ _________________

34) $\frac{5}{7} - \frac{2}{7} =$ _________________

35) $\frac{3}{6} - \frac{1}{6} =$ _________________

36) $\frac{8}{9} - \frac{1}{9} =$ _________________

37) $\frac{9}{11} - \frac{4}{11} =$ _________________

38) $\frac{19}{20} - \frac{18}{20} =$ _________________

39) $\frac{4}{5} - \frac{3}{5} =$ _________________

40) $\frac{3}{4} - \frac{1}{4} =$ _________________

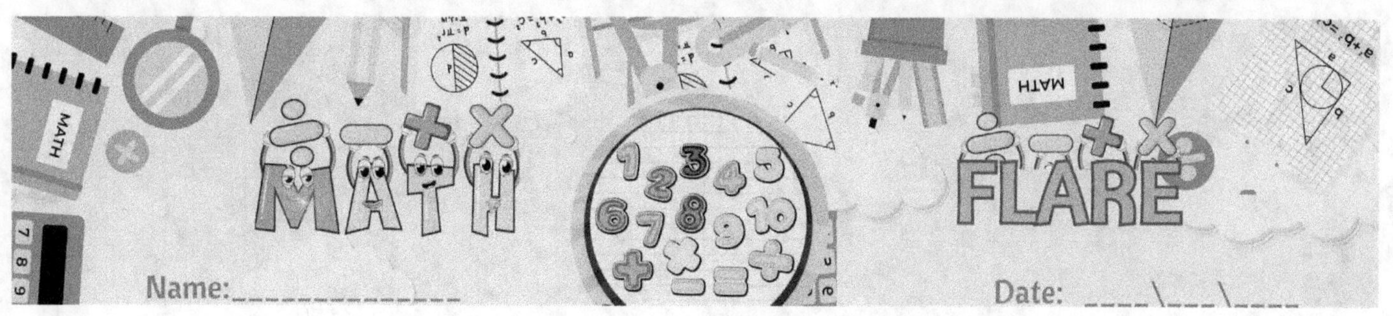

41) $\dfrac{8}{15} - \dfrac{7}{15} =$ _________________

42) $\dfrac{9}{10} - \dfrac{6}{10} =$ _________________

43) $\dfrac{8}{13} - \dfrac{2}{13} =$ _________________

44) $\dfrac{6}{8} - \dfrac{5}{8} =$ _________________

45) $\dfrac{7}{8} - \dfrac{4}{8} =$ _________________

46) $\dfrac{4}{5} - \dfrac{2}{5} =$ _________________

47) $\dfrac{3}{4} - \dfrac{2}{4} =$ _________________

48) $\dfrac{6}{9} - \dfrac{1}{9} =$ _________________

49) $\dfrac{10}{11} - \dfrac{9}{11} =$ _________________

50) $\dfrac{13}{16} - \dfrac{2}{16} =$ _________________

51) $\dfrac{19}{20} - \dfrac{1}{20} =$ _________________

52) $\dfrac{14}{18} - \dfrac{6}{18} =$ _________________

53) $\dfrac{5}{10} - \dfrac{4}{10} =$ _________________

54) $\dfrac{5}{6} - \dfrac{4}{6} =$ _________________

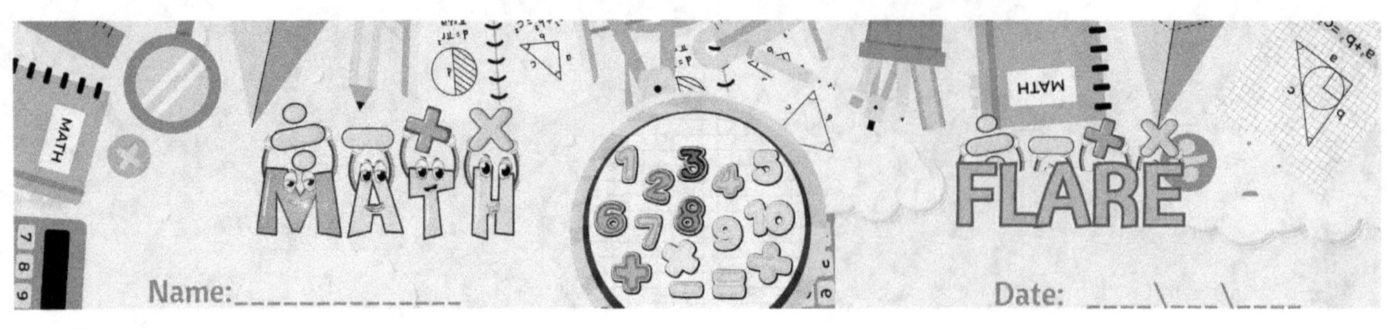

55) $\dfrac{6}{7} - \dfrac{5}{7} =$ _______________

56) $\dfrac{13}{14} - \dfrac{1}{14} =$ _______________

57) $\dfrac{14}{19} - \dfrac{11}{19} =$ _______________

58) $\dfrac{11}{12} - \dfrac{9}{12} =$ _______________

59) $\dfrac{14}{15} - \dfrac{12}{15} =$ _______________

60) $\dfrac{13}{17} - \dfrac{11}{17} =$ _______________

61) $\dfrac{18}{19} - \dfrac{10}{19} =$ _______________

62) $\dfrac{13}{16} - \dfrac{12}{16} =$ _______________

63) $\dfrac{11}{13} - \dfrac{6}{13} =$ _______________

64) $\dfrac{10}{14} - \dfrac{4}{14} =$ _______________

65) $\dfrac{8}{11} - \dfrac{1}{11} =$ _______________

66) $\dfrac{8}{12} - \dfrac{5}{12} =$ _______________

67) $\dfrac{5}{8} - \dfrac{1}{8} =$ _______________

68) $\dfrac{2}{20} - \dfrac{1}{20} =$ _______________

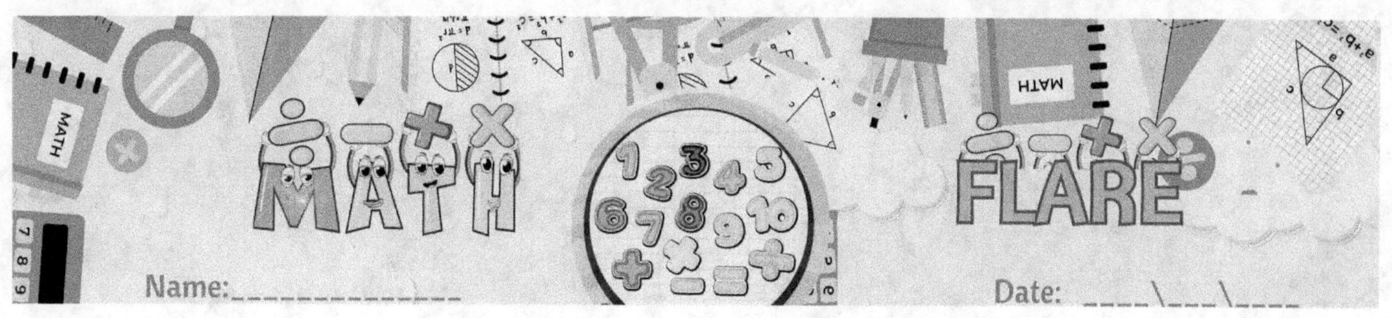

69) $\dfrac{13}{15} - \dfrac{10}{15} =$ _______________

70) $\dfrac{14}{18} - \dfrac{11}{18} =$ _______________

71) $\dfrac{14}{17} - \dfrac{2}{17} =$ _______________

72) $\dfrac{6}{9} - \dfrac{4}{9} =$ _______________

73) $\dfrac{8}{10} - \dfrac{7}{10} =$ _______________

74) $\dfrac{6}{8} - \dfrac{3}{8} =$ _______________

75) $\dfrac{10}{18} - \dfrac{1}{18} =$ _______________

76) $\dfrac{10}{11} - \dfrac{4}{11} =$ _______________

77) $\dfrac{4}{13} - \dfrac{3}{13} =$ _______________

78) $\dfrac{14}{19} - \dfrac{12}{19} =$ _______________

79) $\dfrac{14}{17} - \dfrac{7}{17} =$ _______________

80) $\dfrac{19}{20} - \dfrac{2}{20} =$ _______________

81) $\dfrac{15}{16} - \dfrac{6}{16} =$ _______________

82) $\dfrac{10}{14} - \dfrac{8}{14} =$ _______________

MathFlare - Math Workbook 4th Grade

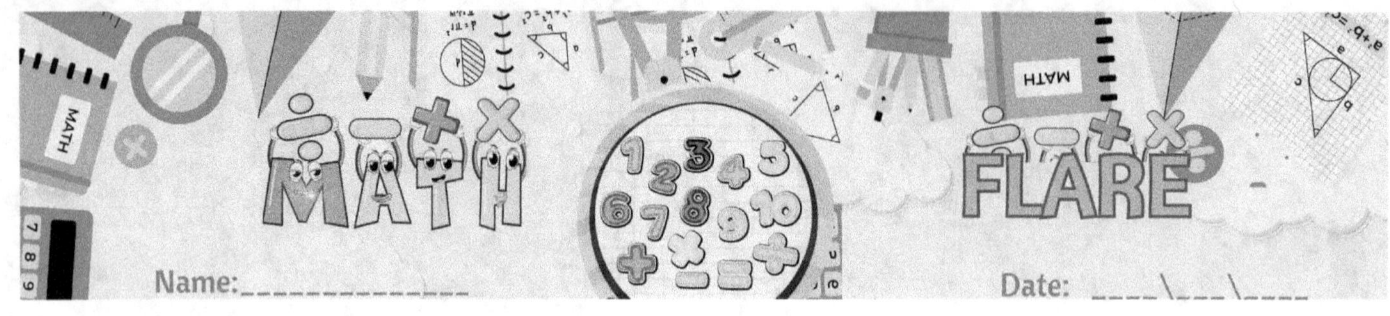

Fractions Multiplication

Find the product.

1) $\frac{4}{5} \times \frac{4}{5} = \frac{4 \times 4}{5 \times 5} = \frac{16}{25}$

2) $\frac{10}{12} \times \frac{4}{12} =$ ________________

3) $\frac{2}{4} \times \frac{1}{4} =$ ________________

4) $\frac{1}{3} \times \frac{1}{3} =$ ________________

5) $\frac{4}{6} \times \frac{4}{6} =$ ________________

6) $\frac{1}{8} \times \frac{6}{8} =$ ________________

7) $\frac{1}{12} \times \frac{4}{12} =$ ________________

8) $\frac{5}{10} \times \frac{8}{10} =$ ________________

9) $\frac{6}{12} \times \frac{8}{12} =$ ________________

10) $\frac{1}{8} \times \frac{1}{8} =$ ________________

11) $\frac{2}{3} \times \frac{1}{3} =$ ________________

12) $\frac{9}{10} \times \frac{4}{10} =$ ________________

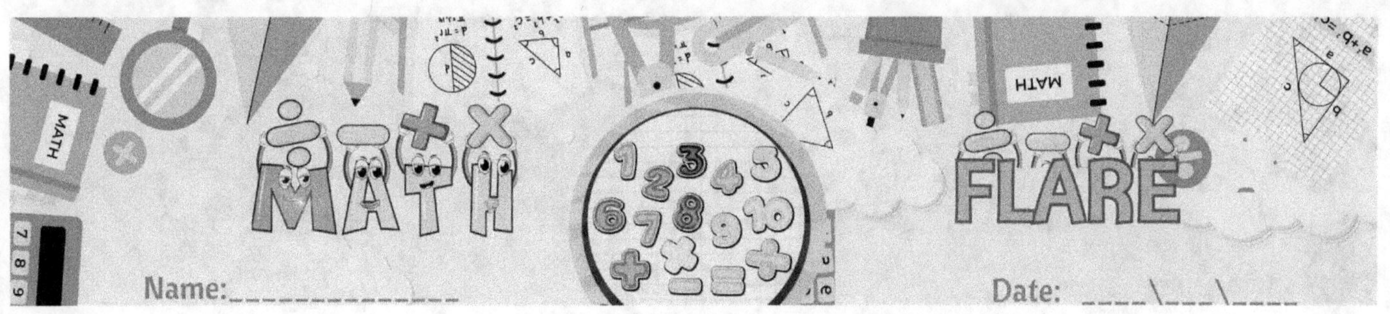

13) $\dfrac{2}{4} \times \dfrac{3}{4} =$ _______________

14) $\dfrac{2}{5} \times \dfrac{4}{5} =$ _______________

15) $\dfrac{1}{6} \times \dfrac{3}{6} =$ _______________

16) $\dfrac{5}{6} \times \dfrac{5}{6} =$ _______________

17) $\dfrac{3}{8} \times \dfrac{1}{8} =$ _______________

18) $\dfrac{3}{5} \times \dfrac{1}{5} =$ _______________

19) $\dfrac{7}{10} \times \dfrac{3}{10} =$ _______________

20) $\dfrac{2}{12} \times \dfrac{8}{12} =$ _______________

21) $\dfrac{11}{12} \times \dfrac{4}{12} =$ _______________

22) $\dfrac{4}{8} \times \dfrac{6}{8} =$ _______________

23) $\dfrac{3}{6} \times \dfrac{3}{6} =$ _______________

24) $\dfrac{1}{4} \times \dfrac{3}{4} =$ _______________

25) $\dfrac{4}{10} \times \dfrac{5}{10} =$ _______________

26) $\dfrac{8}{12} \times \dfrac{5}{12} =$ _______________

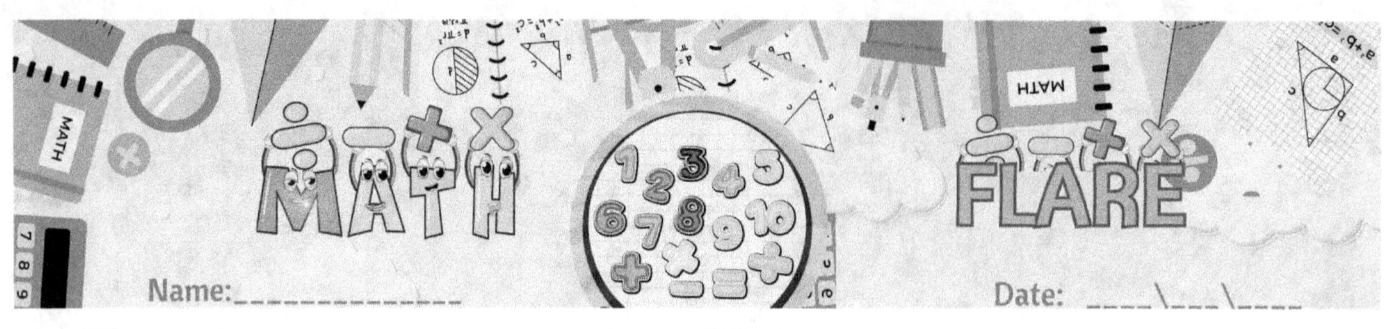

27) $\dfrac{3}{5} \times \dfrac{4}{5} =$ _______________

28) $\dfrac{6}{8} \times \dfrac{7}{8} =$ _______________

29) $\dfrac{7}{10} \times \dfrac{5}{10} =$ _______________

30) $\dfrac{1}{3} \times \dfrac{2}{3} =$ _______________

31) $\dfrac{8}{10} \times \dfrac{7}{10} =$ _______________

32) $\dfrac{4}{5} \times \dfrac{3}{5} =$ _______________

33) $\dfrac{2}{6} \times \dfrac{2}{6} =$ _______________

34) $\dfrac{5}{12} \times \dfrac{4}{12} =$ _______________

35) $\dfrac{2}{4} \times \dfrac{2}{4} =$ _______________

36) $\dfrac{4}{8} \times \dfrac{4}{8} =$ _______________

37) $\dfrac{7}{10} \times \dfrac{6}{10} =$ _______________

38) $\dfrac{3}{4} \times \dfrac{1}{4} =$ _______________

39) $\dfrac{3}{5} \times \dfrac{2}{5} =$ _______________

40) $\dfrac{4}{12} \times \dfrac{6}{12} =$ _______________

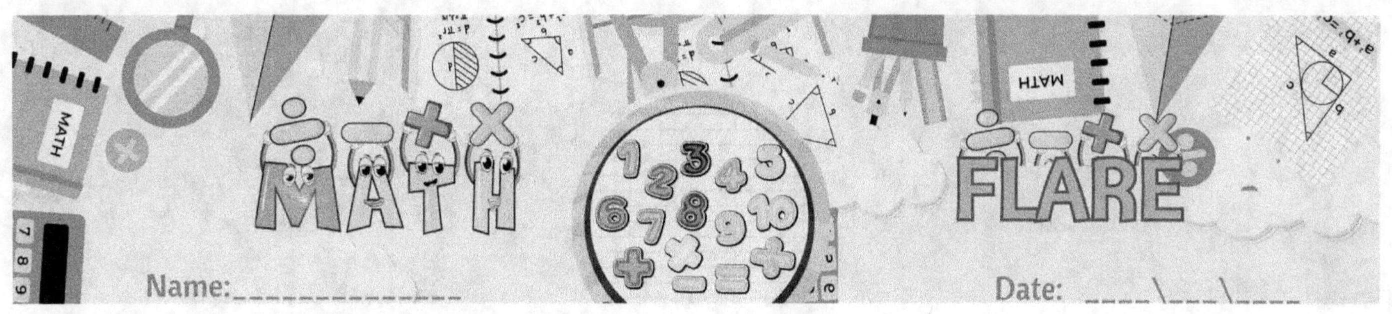

Fractions Division
Find the quotient.

1) $\dfrac{5}{6} \div \dfrac{1}{6} =$ $\dfrac{5 \times 6}{6 \times 1} = \dfrac{30}{6} = \dfrac{5}{1}$

2) $\dfrac{6}{8} \div \dfrac{4}{8} =$ _______________

3) $\dfrac{1}{4} \div \dfrac{3}{4} =$ _______________

4) $\dfrac{2}{10} \div \dfrac{8}{10} =$ _______________

5) $\dfrac{1}{5} \div \dfrac{2}{5} =$ _______________

6) $\dfrac{5}{6} \div \dfrac{4}{6} =$ _______________

7) $\dfrac{2}{12} \div \dfrac{2}{12} =$ _______________

8) $\dfrac{2}{3} \div \dfrac{1}{3} =$ _______________

9) $\dfrac{1}{3} \div \dfrac{1}{3} =$ _______________

10) $\dfrac{2}{5} \div \dfrac{1}{5} =$ _______________

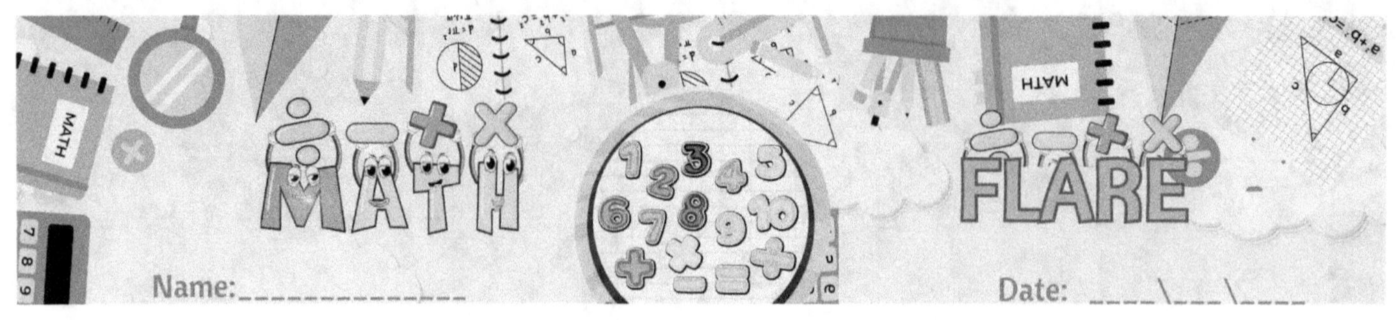

11) $\dfrac{7}{12} \div \dfrac{9}{12} =$ _______________

12) $\dfrac{3}{10} \div \dfrac{9}{10} =$ _______________

13) $\dfrac{2}{6} \div \dfrac{3}{6} =$ _______________

14) $\dfrac{6}{8} \div \dfrac{3}{8} =$ _______________

15) $\dfrac{2}{4} \div \dfrac{2}{4} =$ _______________

16) $\dfrac{1}{3} \div \dfrac{2}{3} =$ _______________

17) $\dfrac{3}{10} \div \dfrac{8}{10} =$ _______________

18) $\dfrac{4}{12} \div \dfrac{5}{12} =$ _______________

19) $\dfrac{2}{4} \div \dfrac{3}{4} =$ _______________

20) $\dfrac{3}{8} \div \dfrac{4}{8} =$ _______________

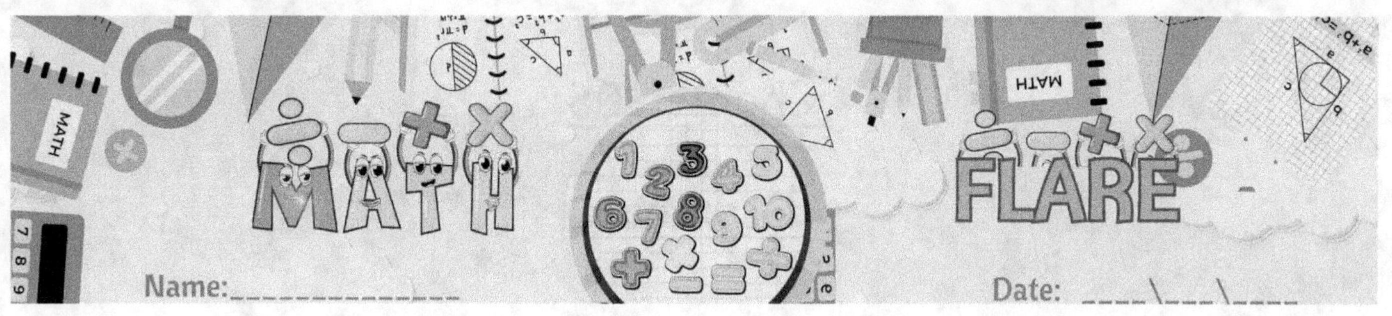

Name:________________   Date: _______________

21) $\dfrac{5}{6} \div \dfrac{2}{6} =$ ________________

22) $\dfrac{7}{10} \div \dfrac{9}{10} =$ ________________

23) $\dfrac{11}{12} \div \dfrac{6}{12} =$ ________________

24) $\dfrac{7}{8} \div \dfrac{1}{8} =$ ________________

25) $\dfrac{3}{4} \div \dfrac{1}{4} =$ ________________

26) $\dfrac{4}{5} \div \dfrac{4}{5} =$ ________________

27) $\dfrac{2}{10} \div \dfrac{6}{10} =$ ________________

28) $\dfrac{2}{5} \div \dfrac{3}{5} =$ ________________

29) $\dfrac{1}{4} \div \dfrac{2}{4} =$ ________________

30) $\dfrac{6}{12} \div \dfrac{4}{12} =$ ________________

Chapter. 06

Geometry

Area and Perimeter

The area of a shape represents the amount of space it occupies. The perimeter of a shape is the total distance around its outer edge.

Area of Rectangle

For a square, since all four sides are equal, we only need to know the length of one side to find its area. We can calculate the area of a square by multiplying the length of one side by itself (squared). So, if the length of one side of the square is 's', then the area (A) is given by:

$$A = s \times s$$

4 in

4 in

$$A = 4 \times 4$$
$$A = 16$$

Perimeter of Rectangle

For a square, since all four sides are equal, we can find the perimeter by adding up the lengths of all four sides. If 's' represents the length of one side, then the perimeter (P) is given by:

$$P = 4 \times s$$

$$P = 4 \times 4$$

$$P = 16$$

Area of Triangle:

The area of a triangle represents the amount of space enclosed within its three sides. The formula for calculating the area of a triangle depends on the type of triangle. For a general triangle, we use the formula:

$$A = \frac{1}{2} \times base \times height$$

Where:

- A represents the area of the triangle.

- The base is the length of any one side of the triangle.

- The height is the perpendicular distance from the base to the opposite vertex.

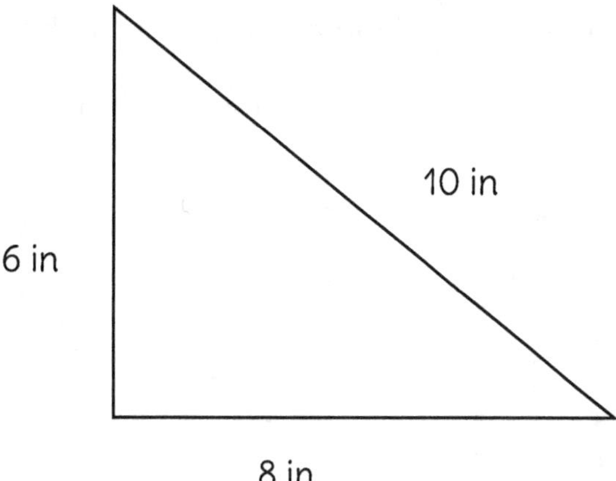

$$A = \frac{1}{2} \times \text{base} \times \text{height}$$

$$A = \frac{1}{2} \times 6 \times 8$$

$$A = \frac{1}{2} \times 48$$

$$A = 24$$

Perimeter of Triangle:

The perimeter of a triangle is the total length of its three sides. To find the perimeter, we simply add the lengths of all three sides together:

$$P = side1 + side2 + side3$$

$$P = 6 + 8 + 10$$

$$P = 24$$

Equilateral Triangle

An equilateral triangle is a triangle in which all three sides are equal in length. To find the area and perimeter of an equilateral triangle, we can use the following formulas:

- Area (A): $\frac{\sqrt{3}}{4} \times a^2$ where a is the length of one side of the equilateral triangle.
- Perimeter (P): $P = 3a$ where a is the length of one side of the equilateral triangle.

Let's solve a problem:

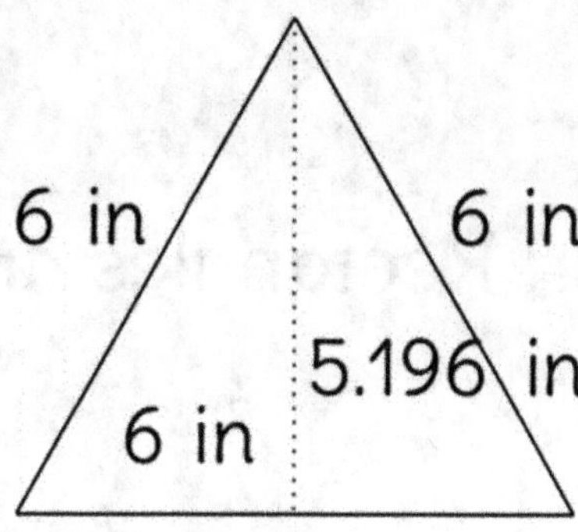

Area of Equilateral Triangle:

$$\text{Area (A): } \frac{\sqrt{3}}{4} \times (6)^2$$

$$\text{Area (A): } \frac{\sqrt{3}}{4} \times 36$$

$$\text{Area (A): } \frac{36\sqrt{3}}{4}$$

$$\text{Area (A): } \frac{36(1.73)}{4}$$

$$\text{Area (A): } \frac{62.35}{4}$$

$$\text{Area (A): } 15.59 \text{ in}^2$$

Perimeter of Equilateral Triangle:

$$P = 3a$$

$$P = 3(6) = 18$$

MathFlare - Math Workbook 4th Grade

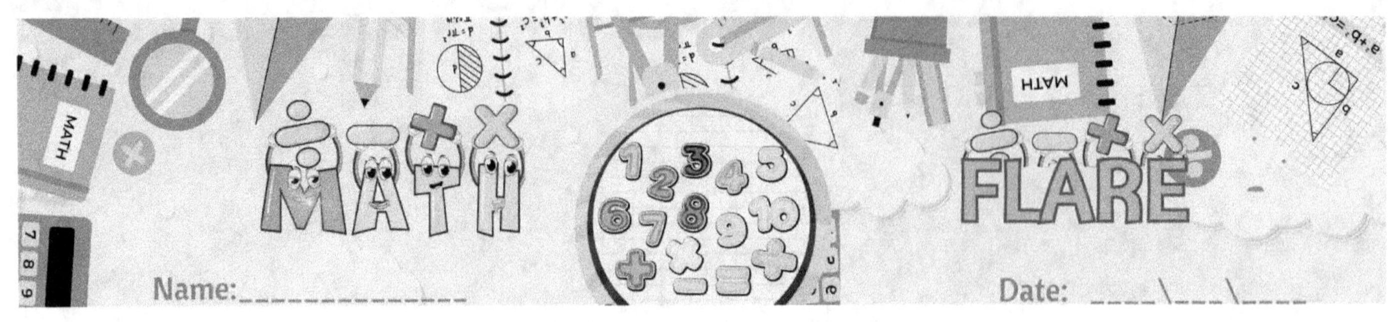

Area and Perimeter: Rectangles and Triangles

1) 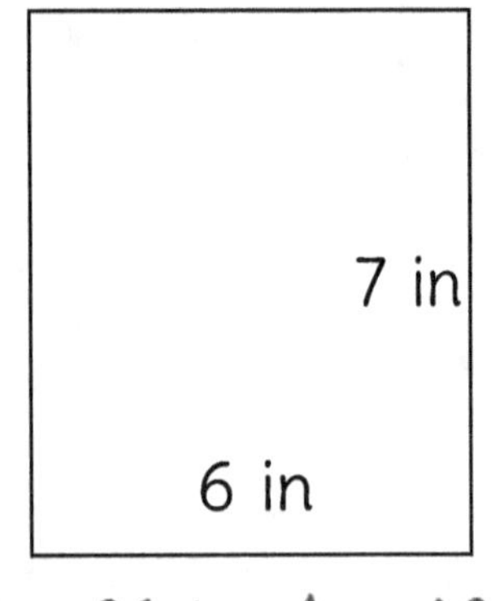

P = 26 in   A = 42 in²

2) 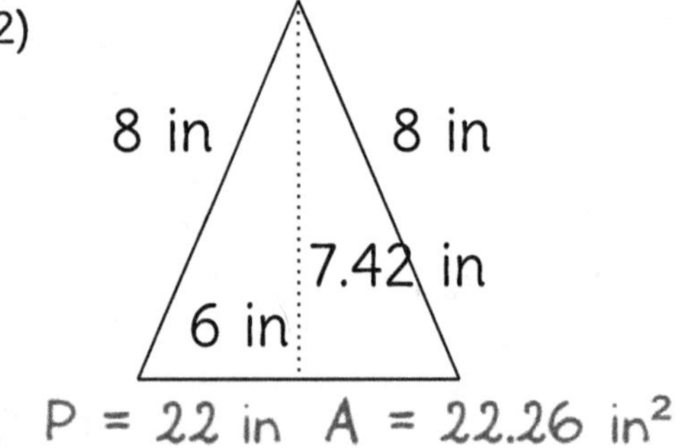

P = 22 in   A = 22.26 in²

3) 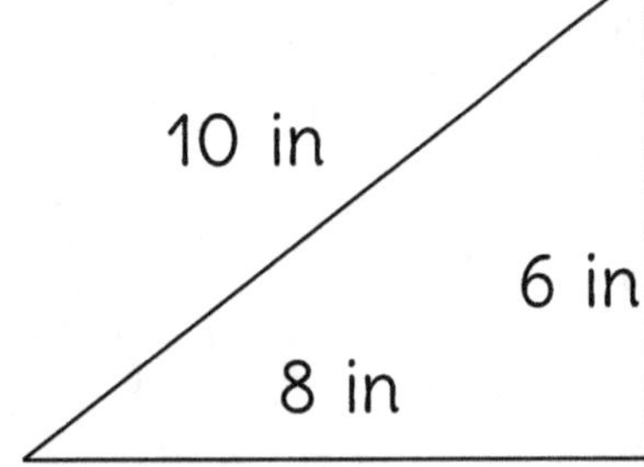

4) 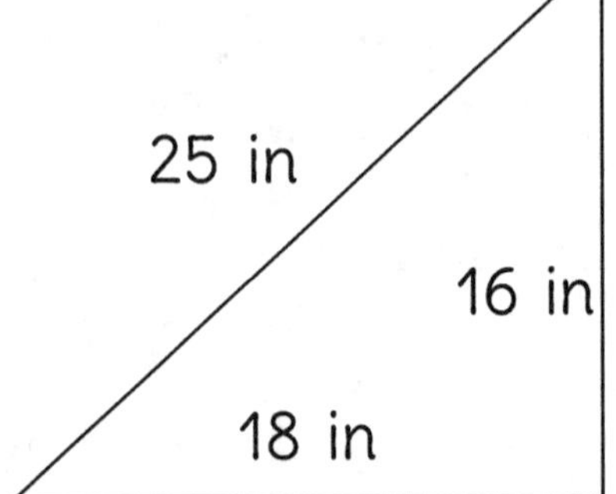

MATH
FLARE
Name:_______________
Date: _______________

5)

8 in
6 in
6 in

6)

8 in
8 in
8 in
6.928 in

7)

8 in
8 in
8 in
6.928 in

8)

15 in
15 in
13.75 in
12 in

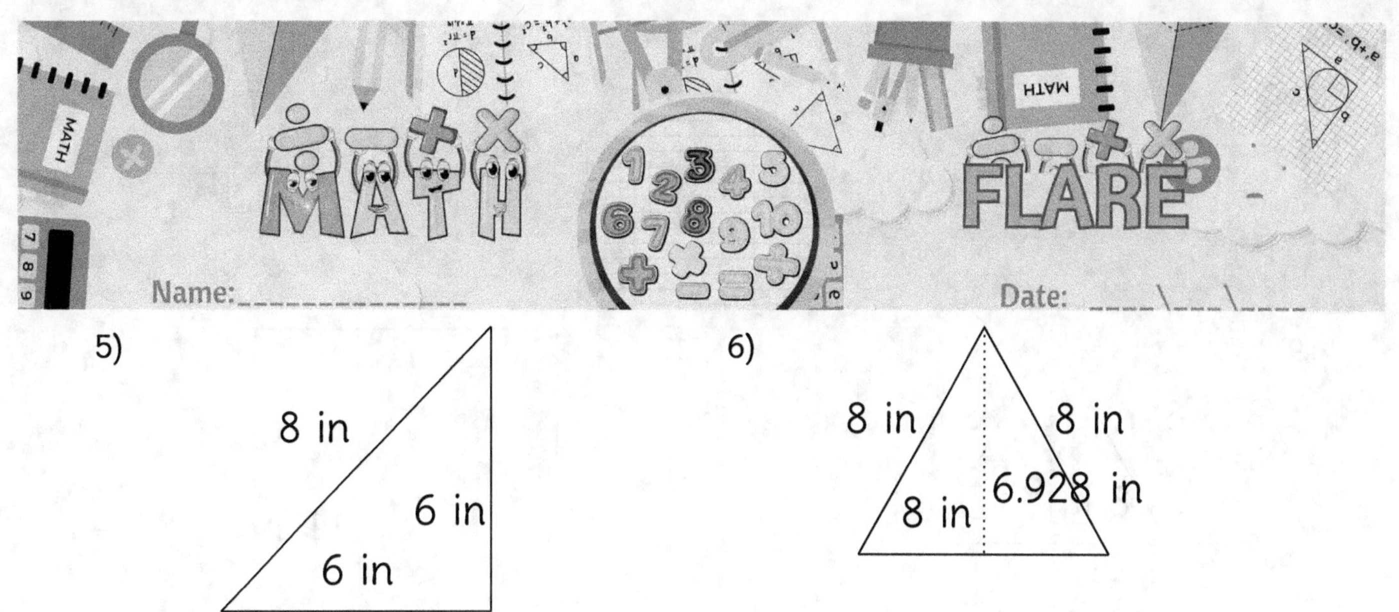

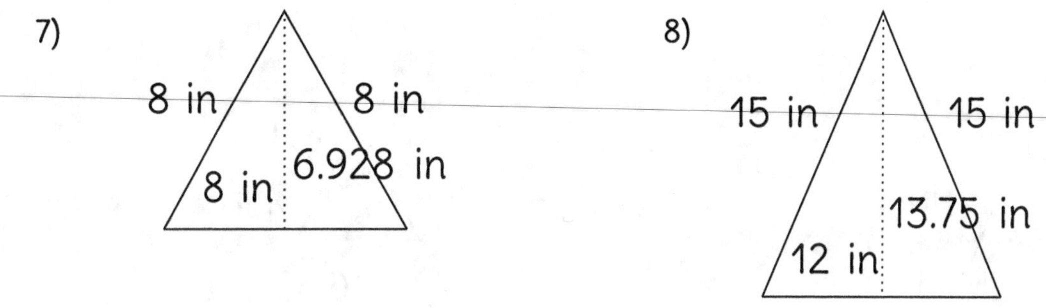

MATH
FLARE
Name:________________
Date: ____________

9)
8 in
8 in
8 in
6.928 in

10)
14 in
11 in

11)
7 in
7 in
6.54 in
5 in

12)
7 in
7 in
6.32 in
6 in

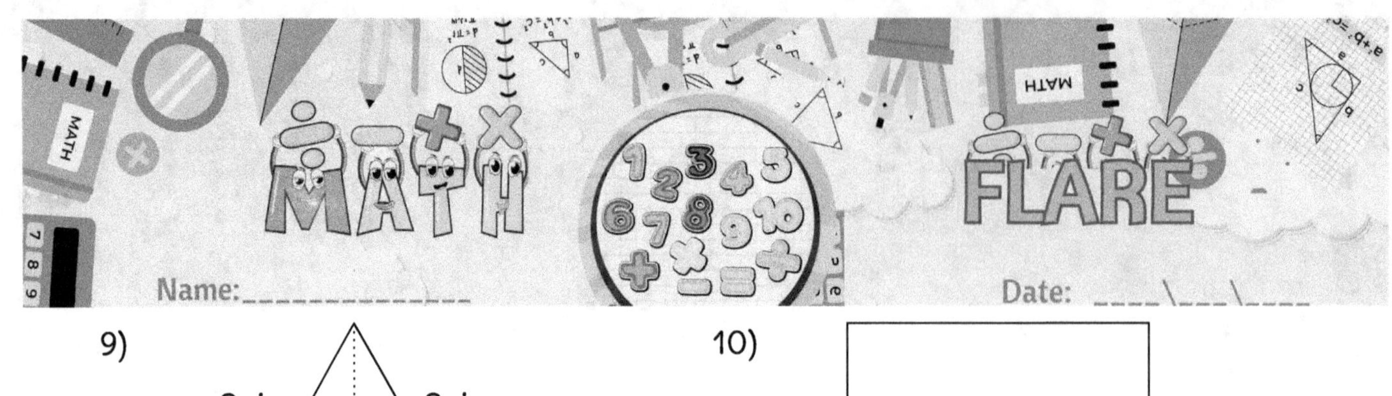

MATH
FLARE
Name:
Date:

13)

7 in
7 in
6.062 in
7 in

14)

12 in
9 in
7 in

15)

11 in
8 in

16)

6 in
6 in
5.20 in
6 in

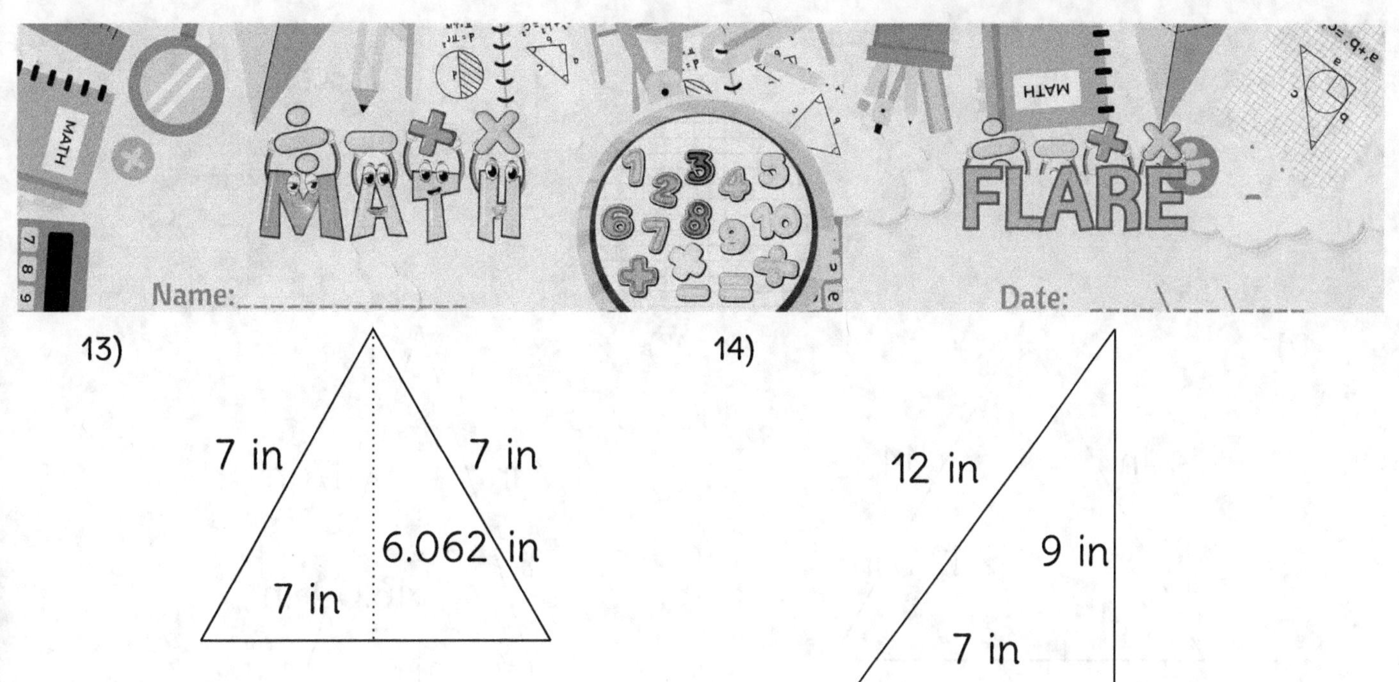

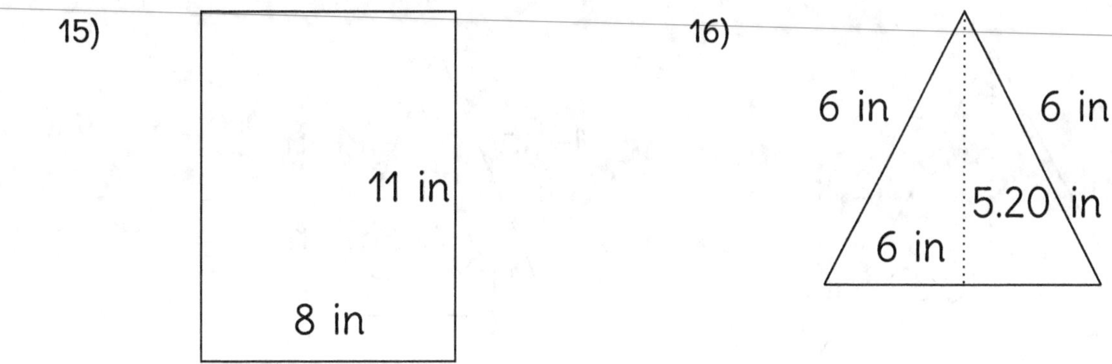

MATH
FLARE
Name:_______________
Date: ____________

17)

14 in
14 in
12.124 in
14 in

18)

17 in
17 in
16.09 in
11 in

19)

12 in
12 in
10.392 in
12 in

20)

14 in
14 in
12.87 in
11 in

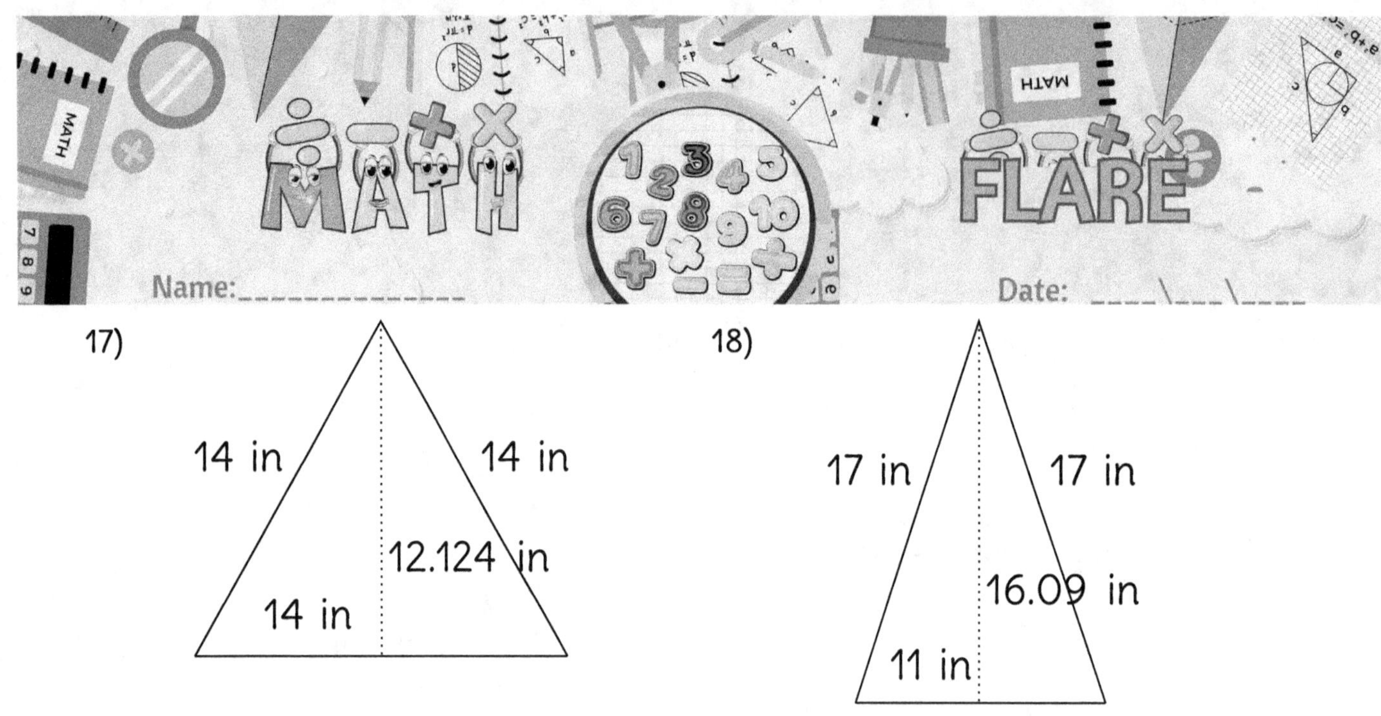

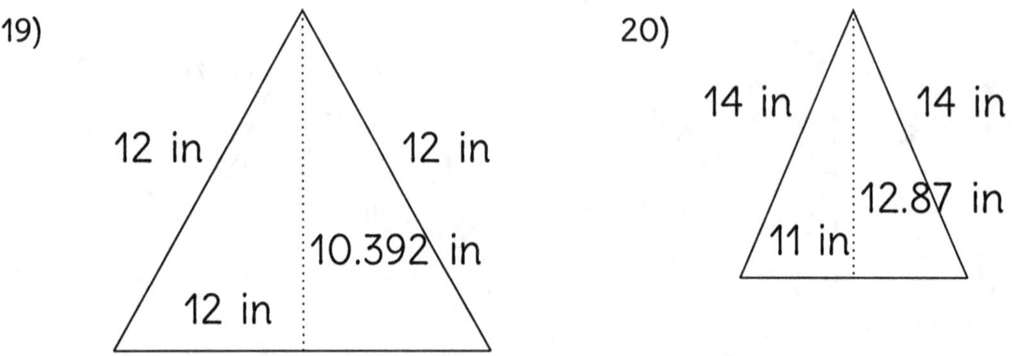

MATH
FLARE
Name:
Date:

21)

22 in
14 in
18 in

22)

15 in
9 in
11 in

23)

15 in
15 in
13.75 in
12 in

24)

7 in
7 in
6.54 in
5 in

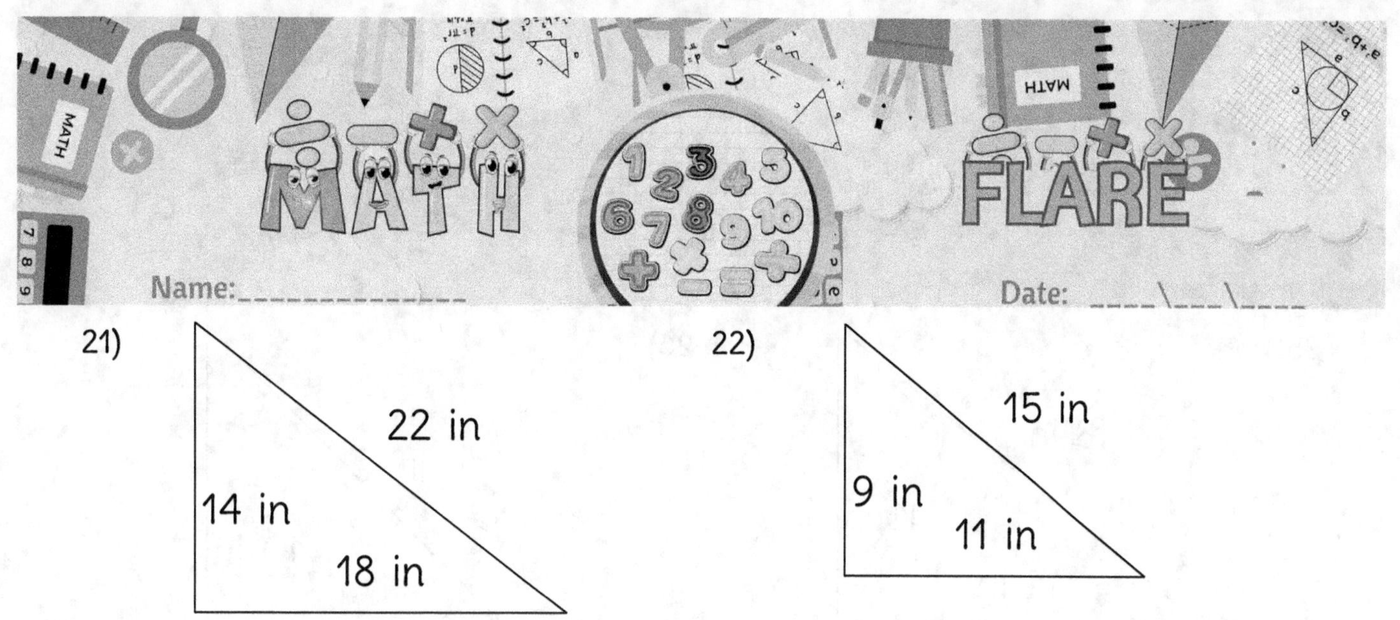

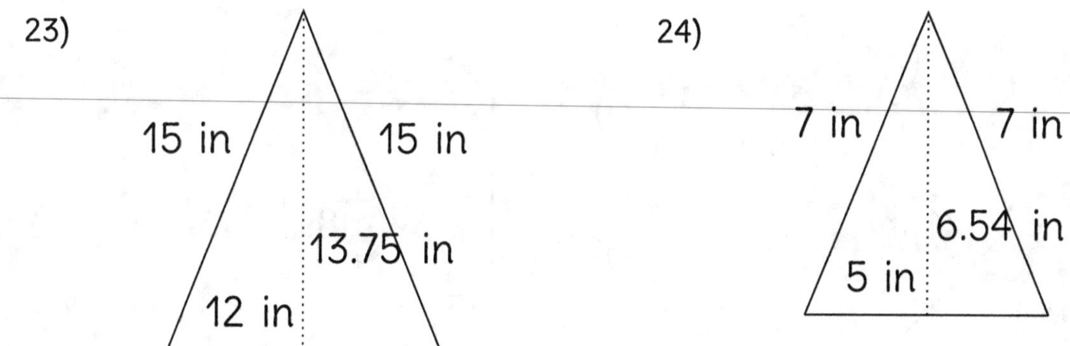

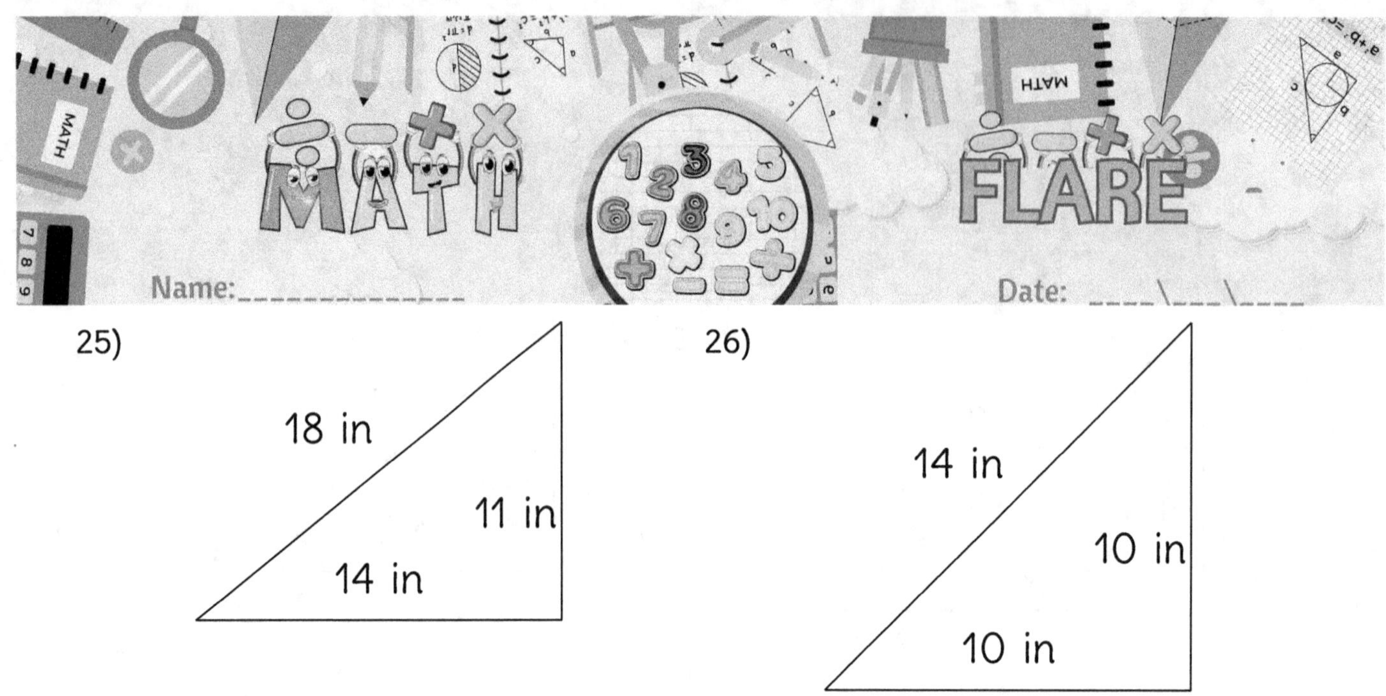

25)

18 in

11 in

14 in

26)

14 in

10 in

10 in

27)

21 in

14 in

15 in

28)

18 in

15 in

11 in

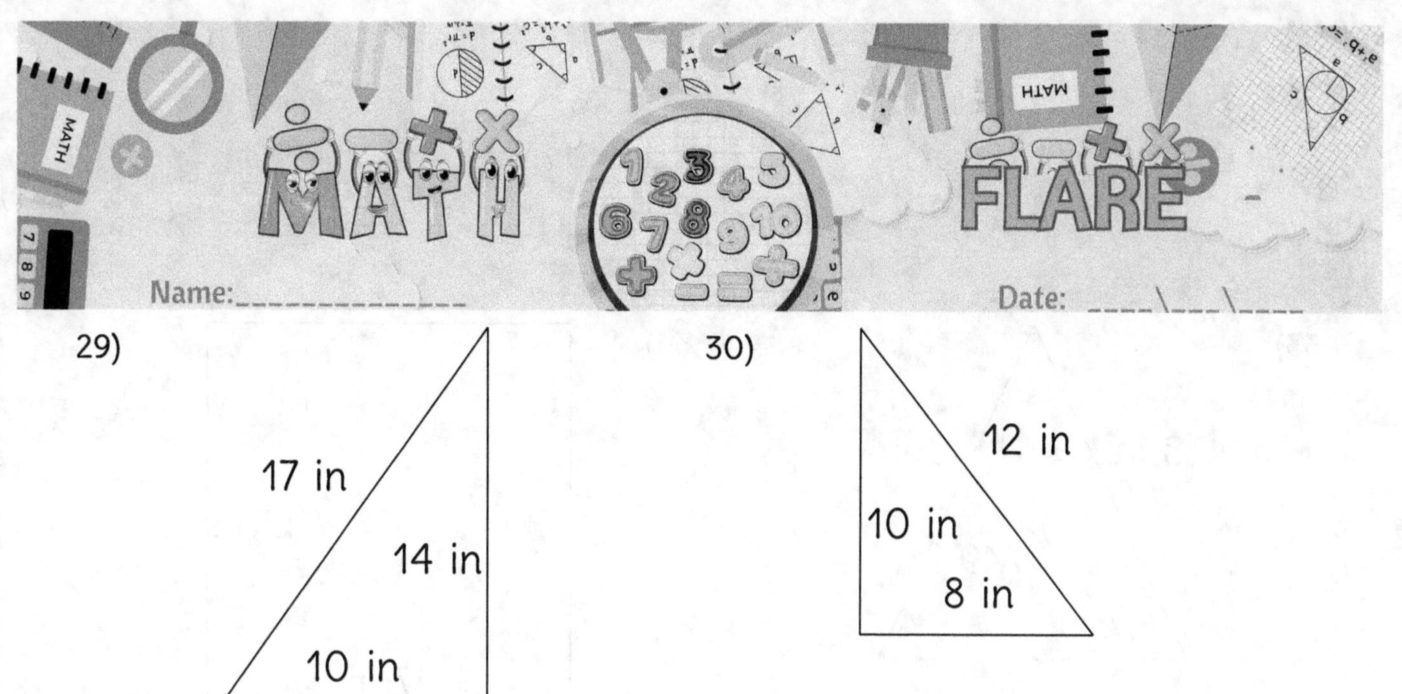

29)

17 in
14 in
10 in

30)

12 in
10 in
8 in

31) 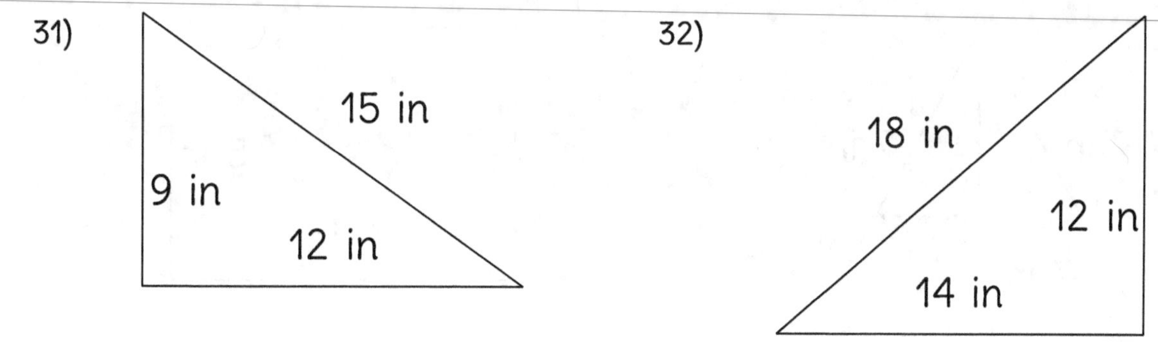

15 in
9 in
12 in

32)

18 in
12 in
14 in

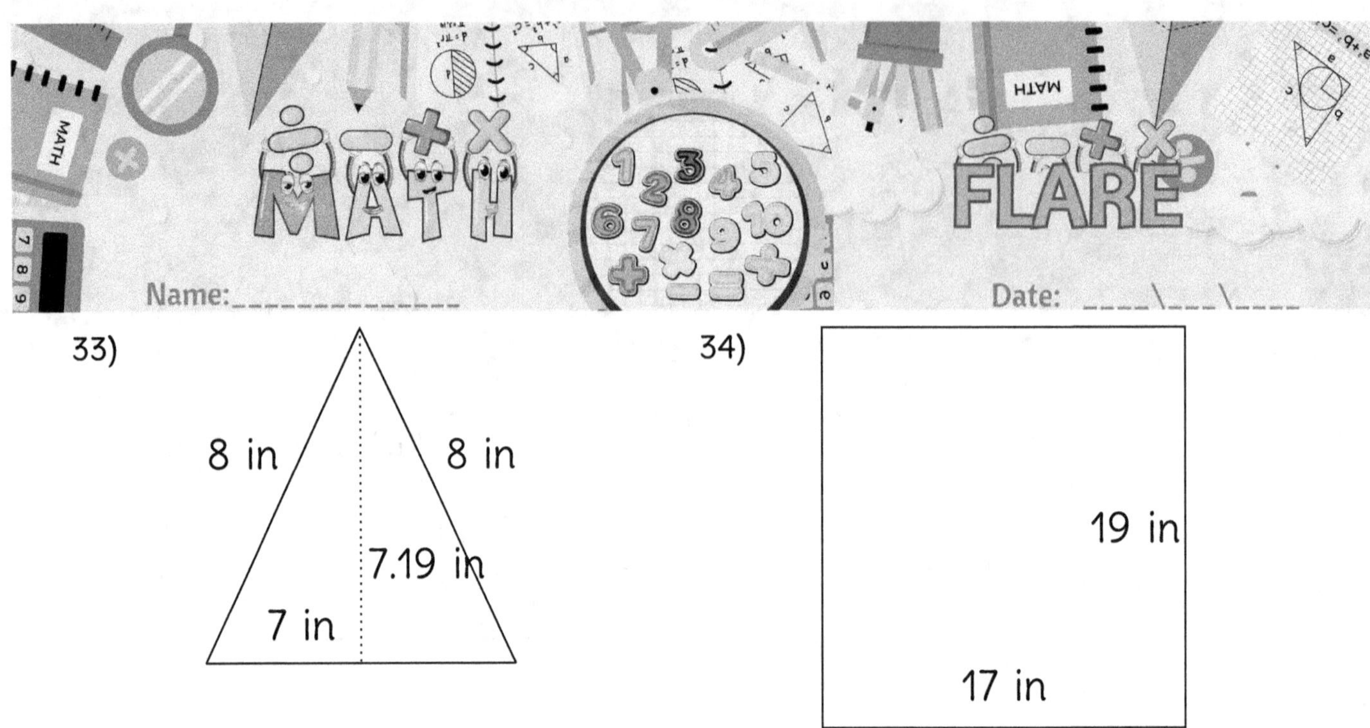

33)

34)

35)

36)

Name:
Date:
MATH
FLARE

37)

11 in
7 in
8 in

38)

7 in
7 in
6.32 in
6 in

39)

17 in
14 in
10 in

40)

11 in
8 in
8 in

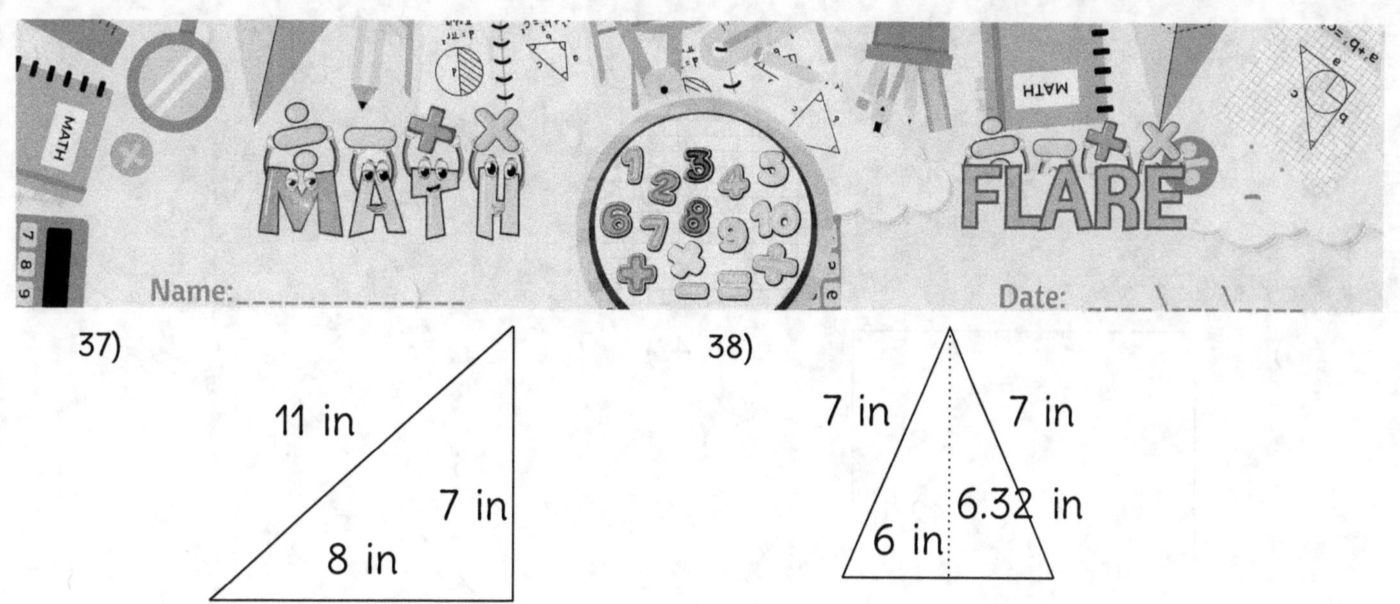

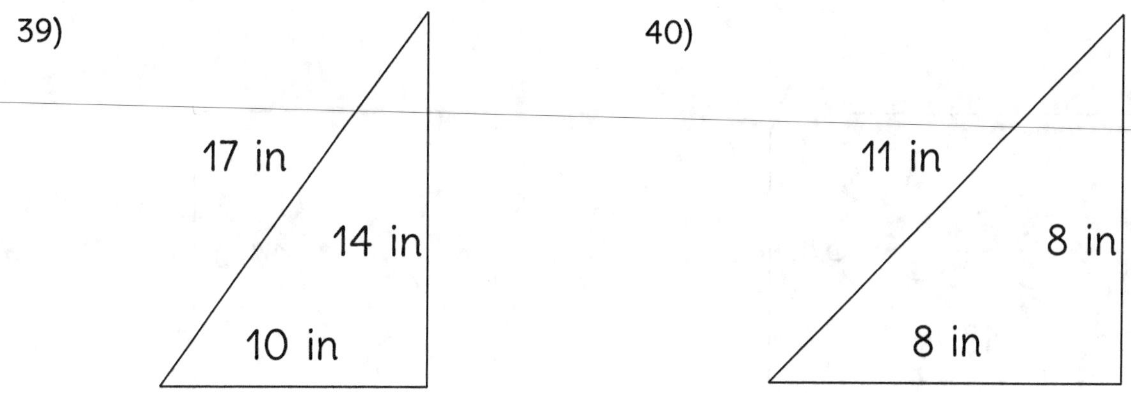

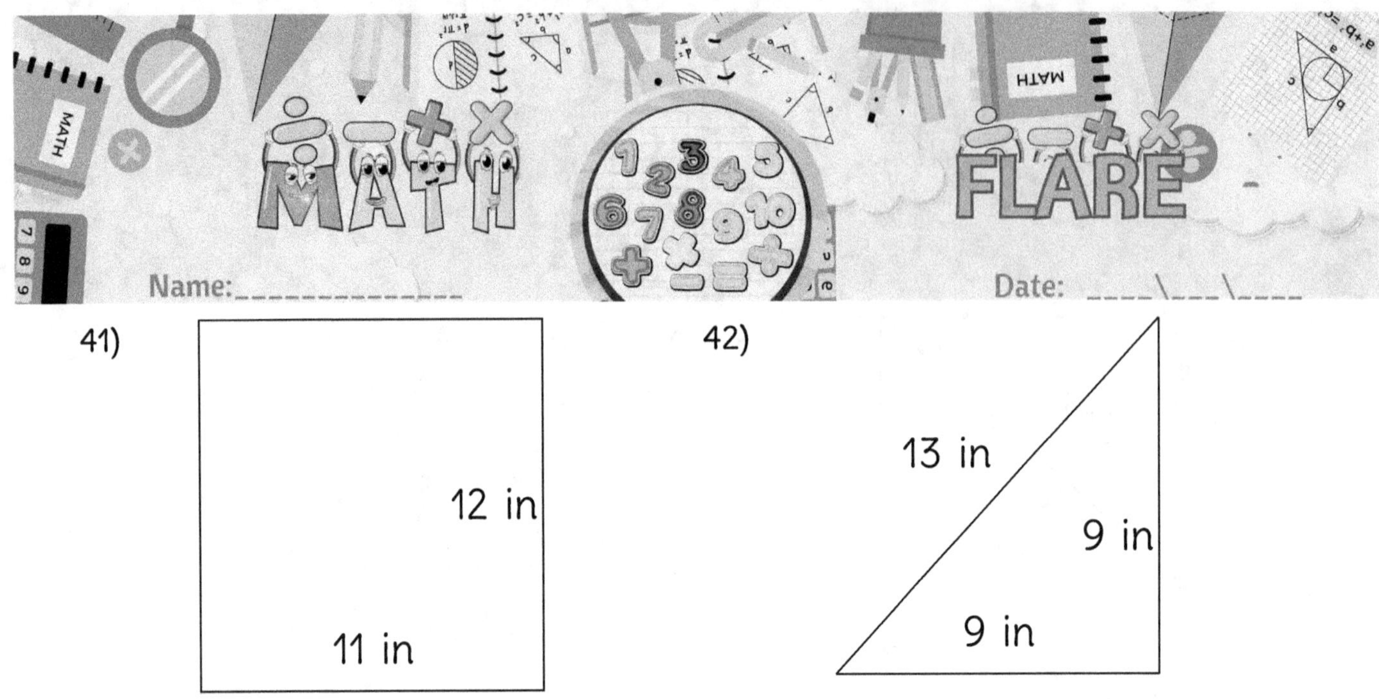

41)

12 in

11 in

42)

13 in

9 in

9 in

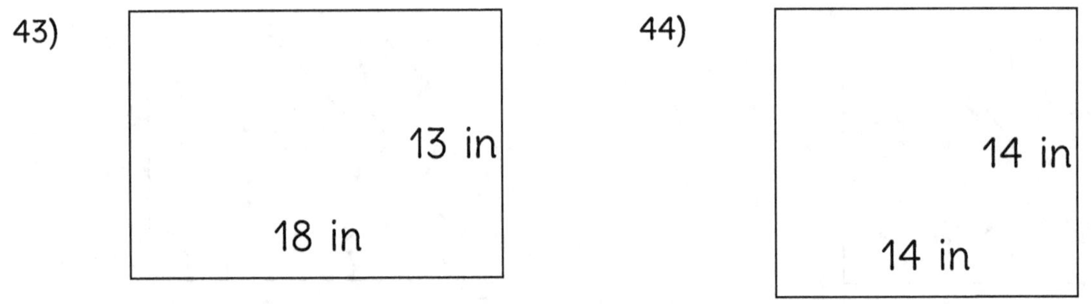

43)

13 in

18 in

44)

14 in

14 in

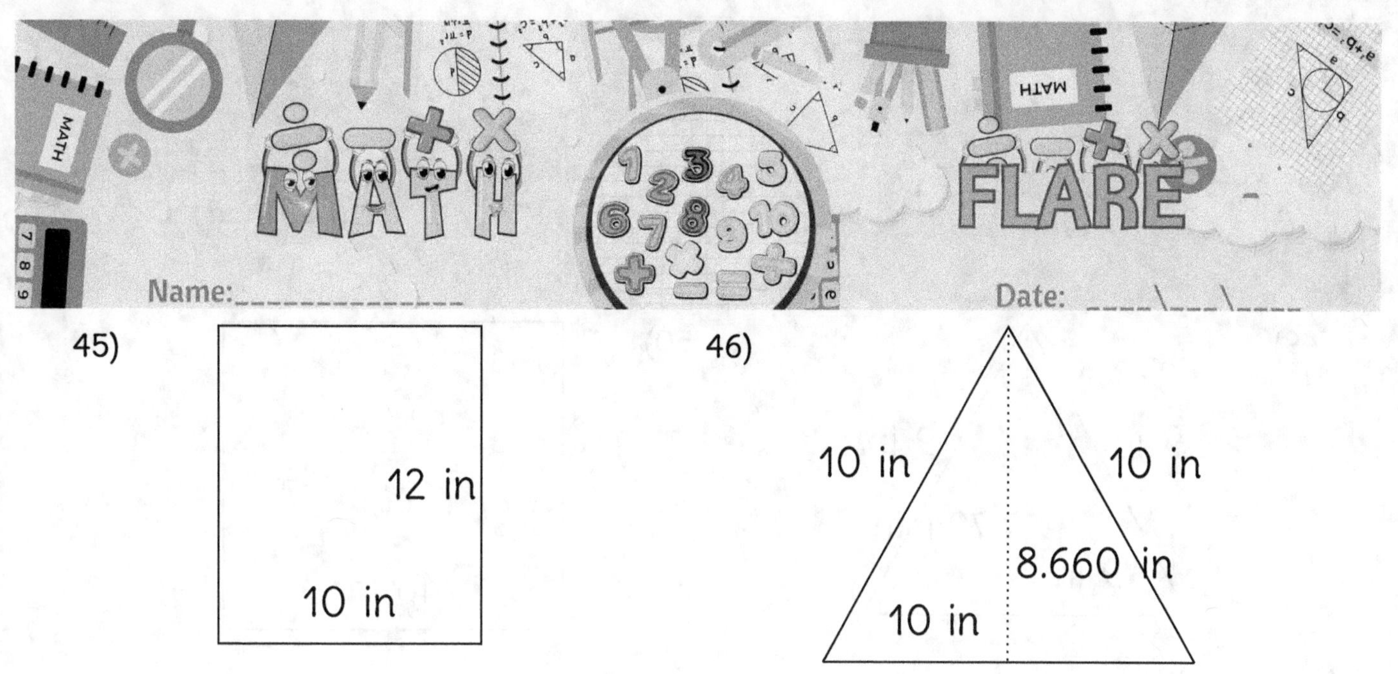

Name:
Date:

12 in
10 in

10 in
10 in
8.660 in
10 in

9 in
9 in
7.794 in
9 in

16 in
16 in

45)

46)

47)

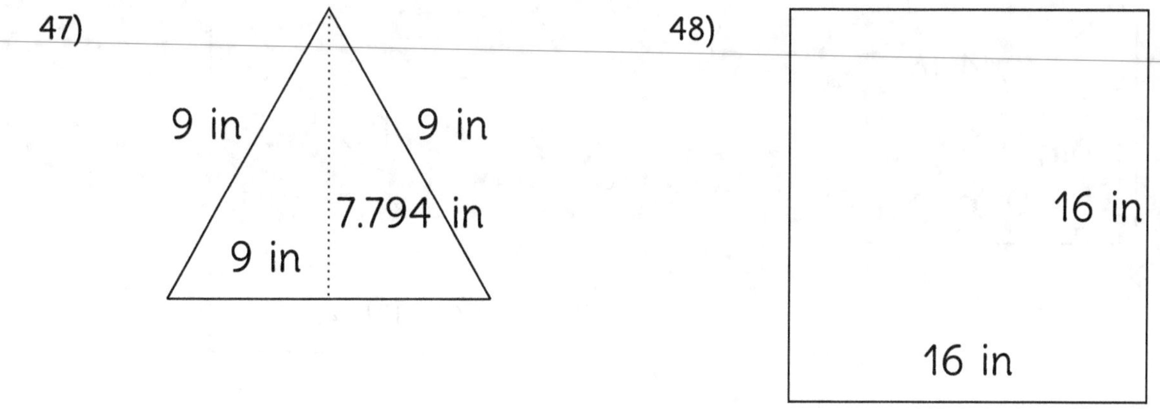

48)

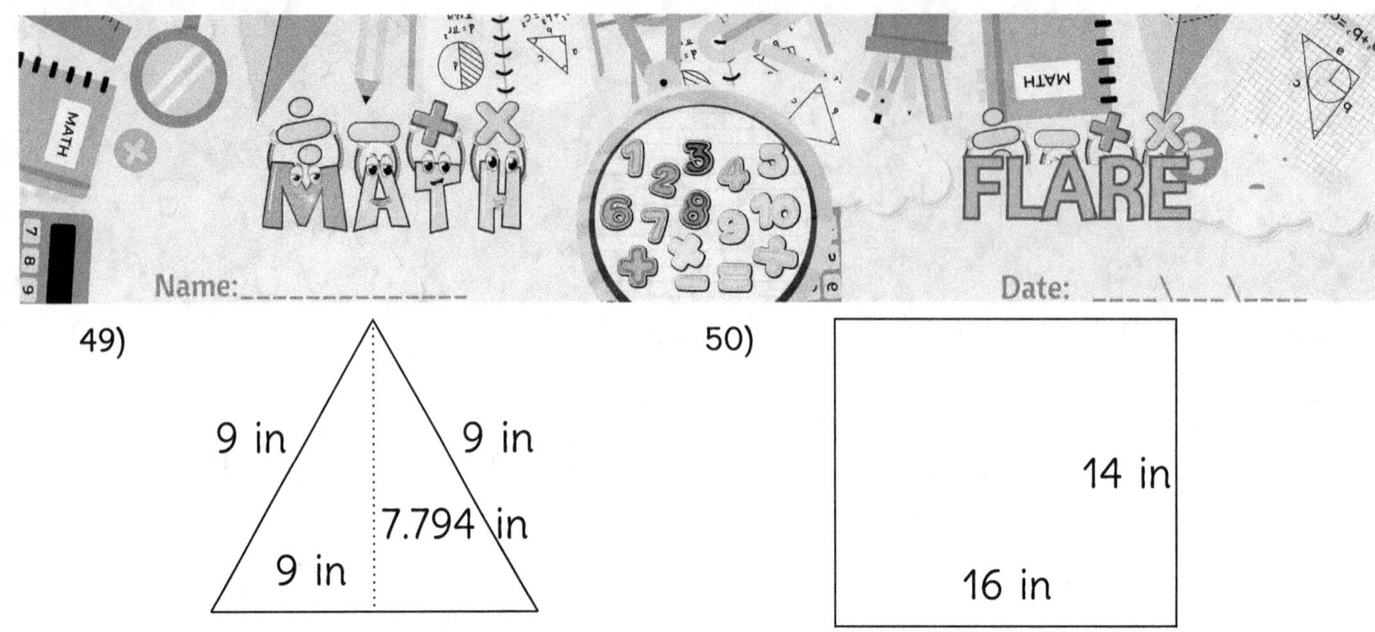

Name:
Date:

9 in
9 in
7.794 in
9 in

14 in
16 in

14 in
10 in
10 in

15 in
12 in
10 in

49)

50)

51)
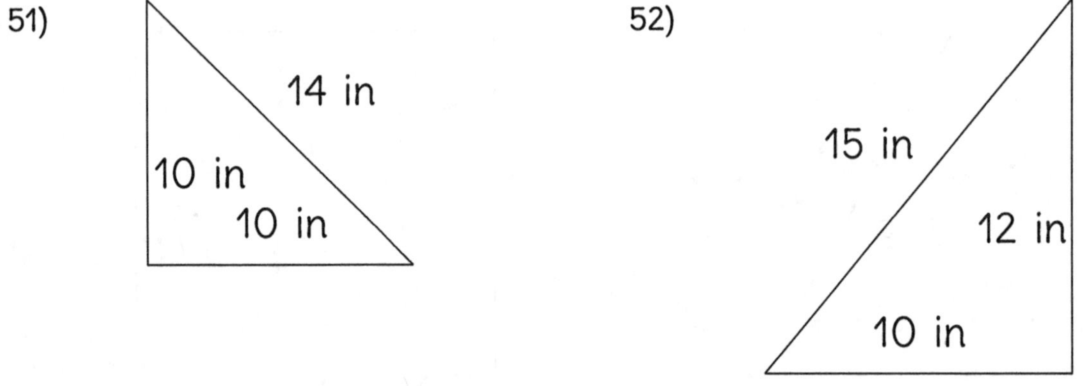

52)

Chapter. 07

Roman Numerals

The table contains the list of roman numerals along with their Arabic number.

Roman Numeral	Arabic Number	Roman Numeral	Arabic Number	Roman Numeral	Arabic Number	Roman Numeral	Arabic Number
I	1	XI	11	XXI	21	XXXI	31
II	2	XII	12	XXII	22	XXXII	32
III	3	XIII	13	XXIII	23	XXXIII	33
IV	4	XIV	14	XXIV	24	XXXIV	34
V	5	XV	15	XXV	25	XXXV	35
VI	6	XVI	16	XXVI	26	XXXVI	36
VII	7	XVII	17	XXVII	27	XXXVII	37
VIII	8	XVIII	18	XXVIII	28	XXXVIII	38
IX	9	XIX	19	XXIX	29	XXXIX	39
X	10	XX	20	XXX	30	XL	40
XLI	41	L	50	LI	51	LXI	61
XLII	42	LI	52	LX	60	LXII	62
XLIII	43	LII	53	LXI	61	LXIII	63
XLIV	44	LIII	54	LXIV	64	LXIV	64
XLV	45	LIV	55	LXV	65	LXV	65
XLVI	46	LV	56	LXVI	66	LXVI	66
XLVII	47	LVI	57	LXVII	67	LXVII	67
XLVIII	48	LVII	58	LXVIII	68	LXVIII	68
XLIX	49	LVIII	59	LXIX	69	LXIX	69
L	50	LIX	59	LXX	70	LXX	70
LXXI	71	LXXX	80	LXXXI	81	XC	90
LXXII	72	LXXXI	81	LXXXII	82	XCI	91
LXXIII	73	LXXXII	82	LXXXIII	83	XCII	92
LXXIV	74	LXXXIII	83	LXXXIV	84	XCIII	93
LXXV	75	LXXXIV	84	LXXXV	85	XCIV	94
LXXVI	76	LXXXV	85	LXXXVI	86	XCV	95
LXXVII	77	LXXXVI	86	LXXXVII	87	XCVI	96
LXXVIII	78	LXXXVII	87	LXXXVIII	88	XCVII	97
LXXIX	79	LXXXVIII	88	LXXXIX	89	XCVIII	98
LXXX	80	LXXXIX	89	XC	90	XCIX	99
LXXXI	81	XC	90	XCI	91	C	100

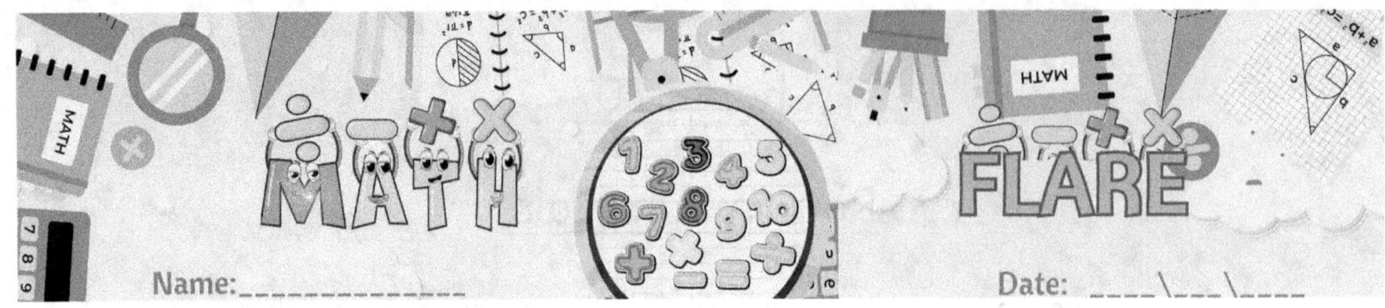

Roman Numerals

1) CXC = _____190_____

2) IV = _____________

3) CCLXXXII = _____________

4) 3 = _____________

5) CLXXXV = _____________

6) VII = _____________

7) LXXII = _____________

8) 32 = _____________

9) 90 = _____________

10) LXV = _____________

11) XCV = _____________

12) LXXIV = _____________

13) XXXIX = _____________

14) CDLXXXIV = _____________

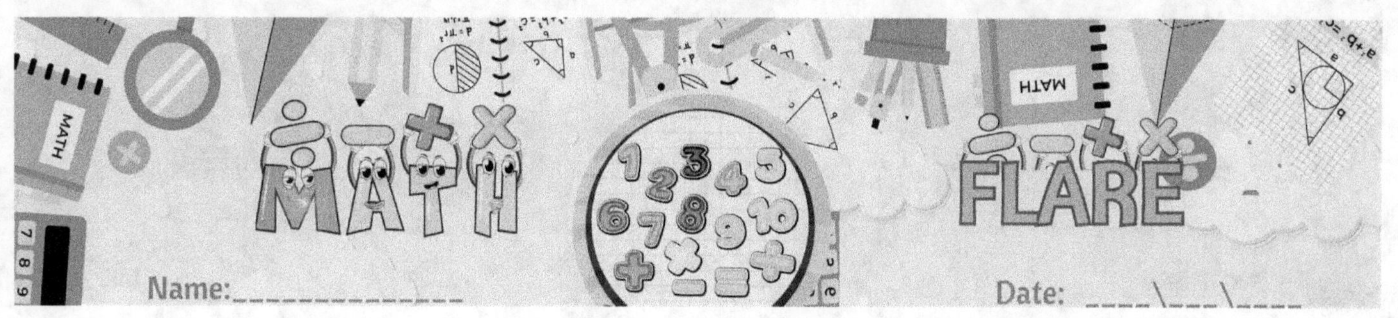

15) I = _______________

16) 60 = _______________

17) CDLVIII = _______________

18) LVII = _______________

19) LVI = _______________

20) 53 = _______________

21) XLVI = _______________

22) VIII = _______________

23) 11 = _______________

24) XXV = _______________

25) 135 = _______________

26) CCCIX = _______________

27) 442 = _______________

28) LXXXV = _______________

29) 356 = _______________

30) XXXVIII = _______________

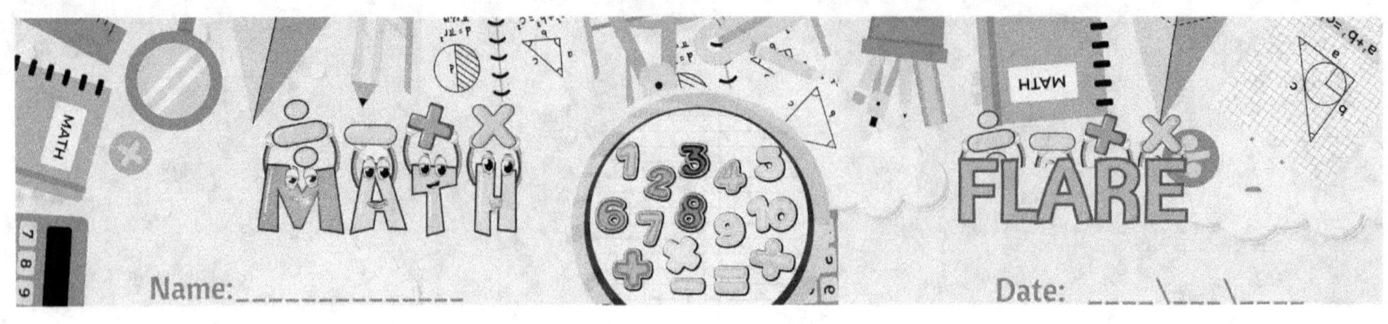

Name:_______________ Date: ____________

31) 109 = _______________

32) 108 = _______________

33) LXXXIII = _______________

34) 2 = _______________

35) 84 = _______________

36) LXVII = _______________

37) XV = _______________

38) XXXVII = _______________

39) 54 = _______________

40) 400 = _______________

41) CCCLXVIII = _______________

42) LXXXVII = _______________

43) 411 = _______________

44) CCCXL = _______________

45) CCCLIX = _______________

46) 286 = _______________

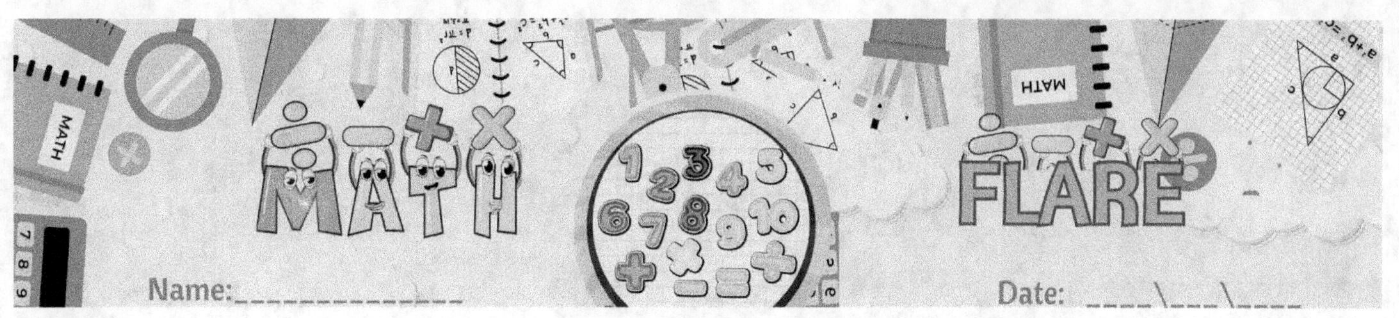

47) 36 = _________________

48) CDXXXVI = _________________

49) XCII = _________________

50) XXII = _________________

51) 315 = _________________

52) XX = _________________

53) CCCXCIV = _________________

54) CCCLV = _________________

55) CI = _________________

56) 23 = _________________

57) XXXV = _________________

58) CVII = _________________

59) CCCX = _________________

60) 265 = _________________

61) 89 = _________________

62) 421 = _________________

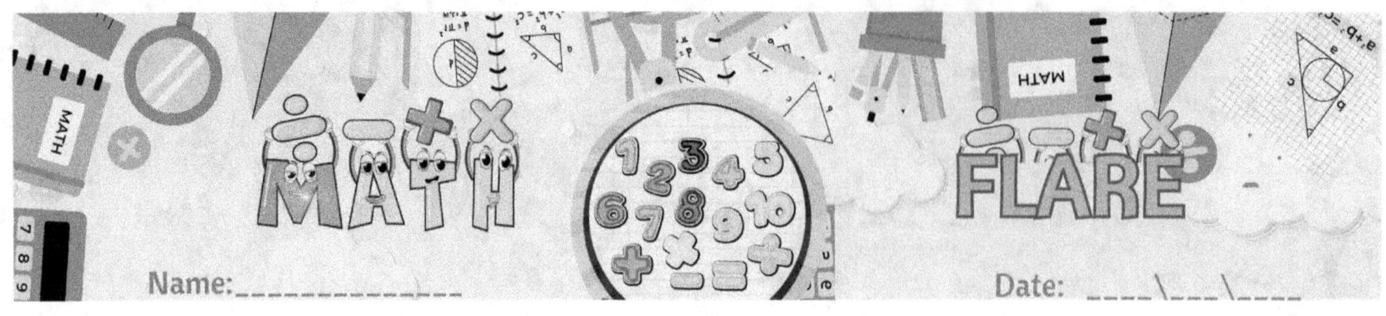

63) XVI = _______________

64) CDXV = _______________

65) IX = _______________

66) 26 = _______________

67) CCLXVI = _______________

68) 94 = _______________

69) 73 = _______________

70) CCCII = _______________

71) XXIV = _______________

72) CX = _______________

73) VI = _______________

74) 457 = _______________

75) CLXXV = _______________

76) 5 = _______________

77) 156 = _______________

78) 333 = _______________

Chapter. 08

Unit Conversion

Metric Conversion
1 meter (m) = 100 centimeters (cm)
1 meter (m) = 1000 millimeters (mm)
1 kilometer (km) = 1000 meters (m)
1 hectare (ha) = 10000 square meters (m^2)
1 square meter (m^2) = 10000 square centimeters (cm^2)
1 cubic meter (m^3) = 1000 liters (L)

Weights and Measures
1 kilogram (kg) = 1000 grams (g)
1 liter (L) = 1000 milliliters (mL)
1 tonne (t) = 1000 kilograms (kg)
1 centimeter (cm) = 10 millimeters (mm)
1 gram (g) = 1000 milligrams (mg)
1 kilometer (km) = 100000 centimeters (cm)

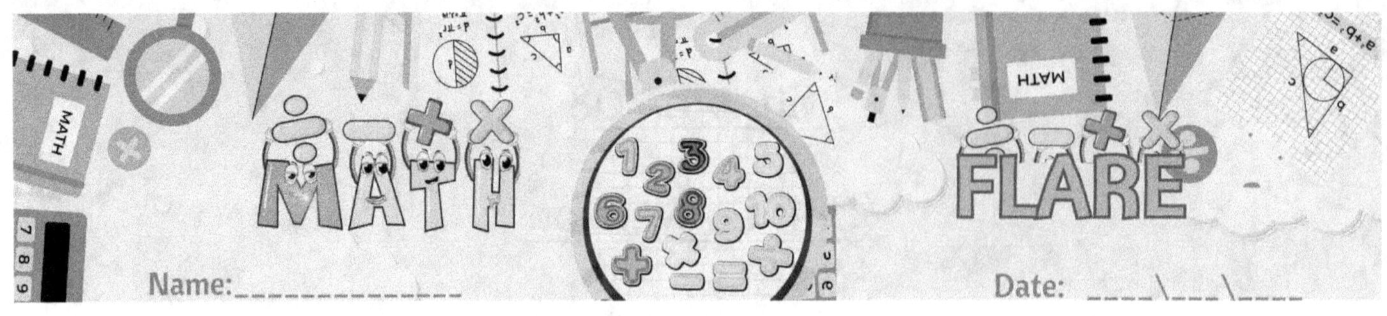

Metric Weights and Measures

Convert the given measures to new units.

1) 88 kL = _88,000,000_ mL

2) 69 m = __________ km

3) 72 cm = __________ km

4) 73 g = __________ t

5) 78 t = __________ kg

6) 22 g = __________ t

7) 26 L = __________ kL

8) 21 kg = __________ t

9) 36 g = __________ t

10) 30 t = __________ kg

11) 47 g = __________ kg

12) 90 kL = __________ L

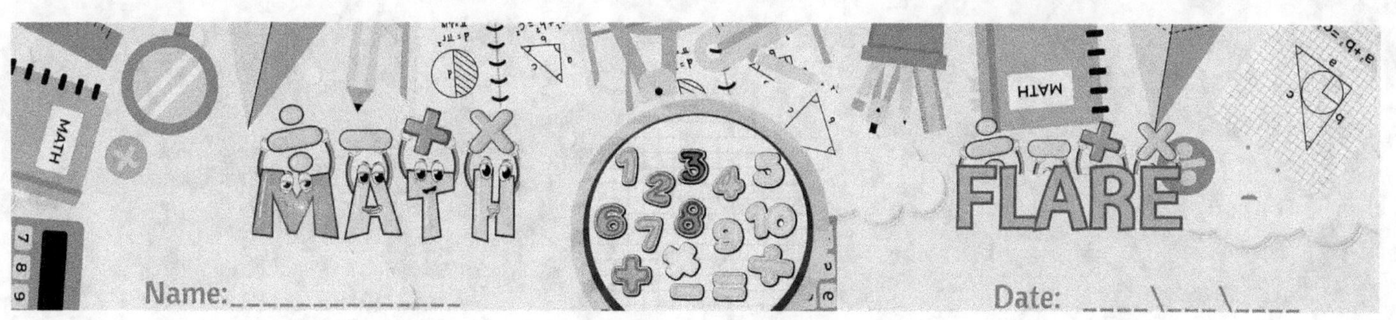

13) 72 kg = _________________ t

14) 88 L = _________________ kL

15) 69 t = _________________ g

16) 11 kg = _________________ t

17) 85 cm = _________________ m

18) 52 g = _________________ kg

19) 25 g = _________________ kg

20) 92 L = _________________ mL

21) 26 m = _________________ cm

22) 28 g = _________________ t

23) 23 km = _________________ cm

24) 37 mL = _________________ kL

25) 70 g = _________________ t

26) 55 km = _________________ m

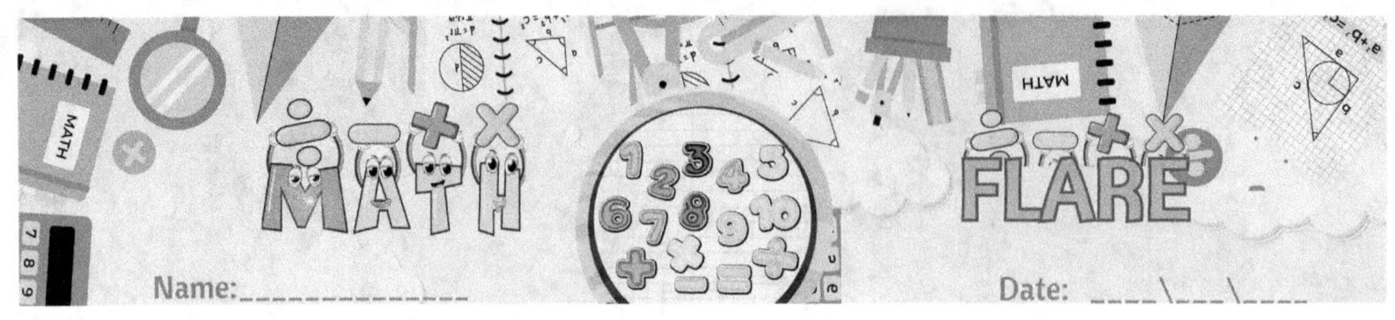

27) 63 kg = ________________ g

28) 85 cm = ________________ km

29) 62 cm = ________________ km

30) 24 g = ________________ t

31) 74 kL = ________________ mL

32) 92 km = ________________ cm

33) 17 kg = ________________ g

34) 80 g = ________________ kg

35) 34 km = ________________ m

36) 52 mL = ________________ L

37) 39 cm = ________________ km

38) 21 L = ________________ mL

39) 50 m = ________________ km

40) 27 m = ________________ km

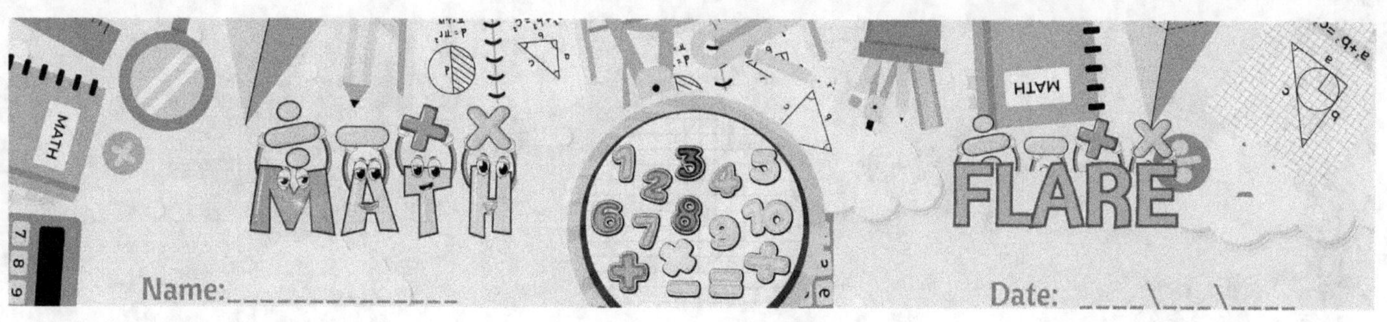

Metric Conversion

Convert the given measures.

1) 26 in = _____0.660_____ m   2) 31 in = _____________ m

3) 60 ft = _____________ m   4) 69 in = _____________ m

5) 97 in = _____________ m   6) 80 ft = _____________ m

7) 15 ft = _____________ m   8) 28 ft = _____________ m

9) 81 ft = _____________ m   10) 50 ft = _____________ m

11) 12 ft = _____________ m   12) 83 in = _____________ m

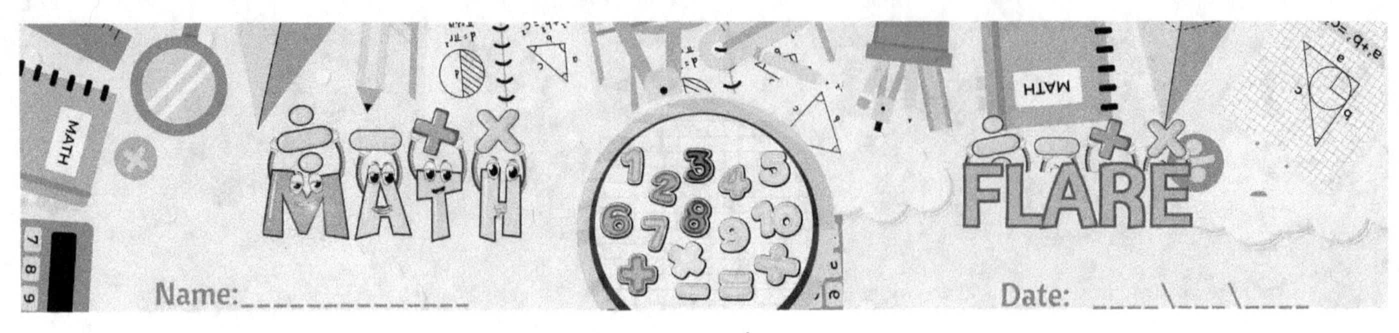

13) 10 in = ___________ m

14) 76 in = ___________ m

15) 42 in = ___________ m

16) 70 in = ___________ m

17) 56 ft = ___________ m

18) 45 ft = ___________ m

19) 13 ft = ___________ m

20) 33 in = ___________ m

21) 58 in = ___________ m

22) 39 in = ___________ m

23) 58 in = ___________ m

24) 23 in = ___________ m

25) 56 ft = ___________ m

26) 54 ft = ___________ m

27) 83 ft = _______________ m   28) 91 in = _______________ m

29) 64 in = _______________ m   30) 27 ft = _______________ m

31) 71 in = _______________ m   32) 74 ft = _______________ m

33) 12 ft = _______________ m   34) 97 in = _______________ m

35) 76 ft = _______________ m   36) 95 in = _______________ m

37) 67 ft = _______________ m   38) 53 in = _______________ m

39) 40 ft = _______________ m   40) 89 ft = _______________ m

ANSWERS

Page 1:   Addition with Regrouping

1. 66,150	2. 58,177	3. 65,412	4. 45,310
5. 81,248	6. 62,110	7. 101,416	8. 41,130
9. 66,343	10. 25,111	11. 71,114	12. 82,433
13. 82,124	14. 42,130	15. 48,212	16. 91,113
17. 45,213	18. 38,765	19. 81,320	20. 94,322
21. 84,422	22. 62,260	23. 79,126	24. 102,110
25. 71,125	26. 22,112	27. 91,120	28. 74,474
29. 101,260	30. 23,311	31. 33,211	32. 51,411
33. 32,250	34. 51,351	35. 33,120	36. 81,212
37. 91,720	38. 92,540	39. 101,210	40. 26,120
41. 42,840	42. 92,511	43. 83,110	44. 31,274
45. 66,118	46. 107,124	47. 75,284	48. 67,223
49. 66,121	50. 103,526	51. 73,111	52. 22,224
53. 61,511	54. 65,110	55. 44,350	56. 43,620
57. 72,110	58. 31,630	59. 25,252	60. 25,210
61. 41,118	62. 41,224	63. 53,340	64. 31,232
65. 98,520	66. 31,316	67. 76,261	68. 33,910
69. 101,255	70. 82,750	71. 101,132	72. 101,620

73. 86,411   74. 55,534   75. 51,113   76. 81,210

77. 71,115   78. 94,111   79. 102,545   80. 91,724

81. 32,910   82. 71,214   83. 71,136   84. 81,317

85. 32,412   86. 41,311   87. 63,112   88. 91,170

89. 41,345   90. 52,230   91. 46,350   92. 105,230

93. 41,426   94. 81,132   95. 21,435   96. 36,123

97. 94,424   98. 44,163   99. 31,513   100. 107,320

Page 6: Subtraction with Regrouping

1. 89,737   2. 19,383   3. 17,877   4. 80,869   5. 42,786

6. 24,684   7. 59,464   8. 45,884   9. 27,266   10. 4,463

11. 34,841   12. 62,867   13. 82,683   14. 58,868   15. 36,838

16. 46,846   17. 54,856   18. 72,887   19. 60,783   20. 31,831

21. 86,474   22. 91,452   23. 44,863   24. 35,784   25. 43,787

26. 51,644   27. 59,876   28. 41,858   29. 7,387   30. 42,671

31. 67,789   32. 59,885   33. 72,888   34. 69,875   35. 27,874

36. 68,864   37. 75,484   38. 84,827   39. 27,244   40. 97,675

41. 85,883   42. 10,762   43. 61,782   44. 8,744   45. 24,844

46. 50,275   47. 25,369   48. 26,647   49. 17,681   50. 883

51. 9,527   52. 44,388   53. 18,784   54. 28,682   55. 23,653

56. 42,789   57. 65,527   58. 79,671   59. 32,883   60. 64,279

61. 54,631   62. 74,729   63. 28,534   64. 32,868   65. 79,861

66. 36,466   67. 86,586   68. 91,886   69. 40,886   70. 20,869

71. 21,479   72. 20,484   73. 67,666   74. 29,673   75. 65,588

76. 27,188   77. 7,752   78. 33,879   79. 67,811   80. 34,884

81. 68,781   82. 61,679   83. 48,466   84. 30,853   85. 46,863

86. 40,848   87. 89,337   88. 18,379   89. 22,754   90. 46,753

91. 41,469   92. 53,438   93. 5,859   94. 53,731   95. 73,884

96. 81,741   97. 9,764   98. 7,374   99. 84,177   100. 70,079

Page 11: Adding Decimals

1. 941.76   2. 793.66   3. 1,478.36   4. 1,183.78   5. 1,023.89

6. 840.34   7. 1,248.51   8. 428.29   9. 933.89   10. 1,176.06

11. 577.90   12. 1,099.91   13. 936.72   14. 1,141.48   15. 1,955.69

16. 1,238.37   17. 1,395.66   18. 1,547.64   19. 519.82   20. 1,088.13

21. 928.41   22. 1,107.78   23. 1,459.47   24. 1,162.94   25. 1,527.03

26. 1,249.43   27. 999.49   28. 1,592.31   29. 1,178.24   30. 1,528.50

31. 1,448.69   32. 857.53   33. 800.96   34. 757.32   35. 1,101.39

36. 535.21   37. 1,313.92   38. 1,663.21   39. 1,048.59   40. 1,375.97

41. 1,098.05   42. 877.44   43. 1,082.77   44. 919.96   45. 1,018.67

46. 1,751.40   47. 1,245.75   48. 1,614.54   49. 1,352.17   50. 689.05

51. 572.84   52. 474.76   53. 1,125.99   54. 1,640.07   55. 1,629.52

56. 1,036.76   57. 1,682.21   58. 1,419.29   59. 1,201.84   60. 908.89

Page 14: Subtracting Decimals

1. 22.97	2. 497.29	3. 217.78	4. 474.32	5. 847.22
6. 301.74	7. 54.82	8. 526.67	9. 127.43	10. 17.54
11. 402.88	12. 39.78	13. 473.83	14. 548.07	15. 370.48
16. 686.57	17. 780.84	18. 339.34	19. 228.50	20. 192.90
21. 474.79	22. 396.01	23. 758.40	24. 372.62	25. 494.96
26. 728.29	27. 720.36	28. 718.52	29. 164.18	30. 196.66
31. 178.05	32. 455.27	33. 119.38	34. 206.14	35. 99.37
36. 506.21	37. 602.32	38. 789.25	39. 317.30	40. 563.99
41. 283.30	42. 126.35	43. 20.71	44. 318.04	45. 493.36
46. 442.28	47. 398.69	48. 289.14	49. 471.46	50. 234.06
51. 90.98	52. 114.59	53. 385.80	54. 8.48	55. 228.05
56. 388.54	57. 295.35	58. 13.98	59. 168.59	60. 44.75

Page 17: Addition (3 Addends)

1. 17,362	2. 11,280	3. 23,592	4. 17,648	5. 14,559
6. 14,586	7. 18,344	8. 16,469	9. 19,796	10. 16,619
11. 9,266	12. 26,038	13. 20,438	14. 13,116	15. 14,553
16. 11,893	17. 21,750	18. 16,754	19. 18,560	20. 18,458
21. 17,154	22. 11,041	23. 11,413	24. 14,048	25. 14,802
26. 19,624	27. 17,137	28. 15,930	29. 9,872	30. 16,739
31. 21,964	32. 21,613	33. 9,515	34. 5,717	35. 25,809

36. 18,513   37. 24,466   38. 18,620   39. 18,840   40. 16,063

41. 21,317   42. 15,037   43. 16,719   44. 10,843   45. 20,449

46. 10,582   47. 17,866   48. 22,618

Page 20: Multiplication (double Digit)

1. 7,440   2. 1,566   3. 1,806   4. 3,445   5. 5,950   6. 6,580

7. 4,816   8. 8,930   9. 1,581   10. 990   11. 1,364   12. 5,920

13. 847   14. 915   15. 9,114   16. 672   17. 154   18. 363

19. 247   20. 3,162   21. 825   22. 1,240   23. 3,608   24. 5,916

25. 923   26. 3,432   27. 1,955   28. 3,186   29. 1,073   30. 1,806

31. 224   32. 4,914   33. 2,015   34. 7,650   35. 3,102   36. 4,128

37. 6,417   38. 1,513   39. 4,680   40. 4,095   41. 1,134   42. 2,146

43. 4,182   44. 2,639

Page 23: Multiplication (3 Digit)

1. 418,840   2. 667,488   3. 699,468   4. 50,505   5. 52,323

6. 33,633   7. 421,575   8. 116,640   9. 113,766   10. 888,408

11. 100,932   12. 526,396   13. 336,600   14. 479,896   15. 148,779

16. 244,027   17. 462,384   18. 229,510   19. 33,744   20. 524,908

21. 93,702   22. 458,724   23. 359,625   24. 568,546   25. 316,598

26. 254,100   27. 319,224   28. 789,421   29. 22,952   30. 128,892

31. 179,278   32. 469,270   33. 603,519   34. 451,008   35. 84,152

36. 760,950   37. 79,369   38. 429,408   39. 206,661   40. 258,996

41. 749,736   42. 51,800   43. 84,185   44. 123,072

Page 26:   Multiplying Decimals

1. 107.5417   2. 94.9696   3. 261.8000   4. 85.8480

5. 92.1844   6. 480.1920   7. 430.0992   8. 92.8344

9. 402.9482   10. 739.5300   11. 815.9616   12. 229.8617

13. 570.8664   14. 181.2590   15. 152.5806   16. 185.0438

17. 747.3732   18. 65.6143   19. 539.9572   20. 63.2700

21. 173.9763   22. 348.9692   23. 316.5309   24. 355.9257

25. 702.3625   26. 71.5368   27. 166.0000   28. 90.2645

29. 203.0592   30. 354.0928   31. 394.5496   32. 145.6928

33. 526.7808   34. 140.2300   35. 230.4744   36. 645.8540

37. 436.9270   38. 308.2264   39. 261.1440   40. 112.1766

41. 149.4048   42. 247.4712   43. 156.1396   44. 208.1808

45. 80.0896   46. 821.2045   47. 150.0135   48. 370.2816

49. 245.1960   50. 222.9364   51. 425.7515   52. 215.0040

53. 770.8432   54. 246.2896   55. 271.8792   56. 670.7316

57. 464.2528   58. 259.1844   59. 407.6163   60. 211.3332

61. 540.2502   62. 105.9863   63. 235.0260

Page 33:   Dividing Decimals

1. 0.94   2. 1.35   3. 1.64   4. 0.95   5. 1.85   6. 0.66   7. 0.35

8. 1.83   9. 2.75   10. 0.55   11. 1.09   12. 1.37   13. 1.25   14. 0.64

15. 0.22   16. 1.47   17. 1.83   18. 1   19. 0.29   20. 0.96   21. 1.72

22. 0.36   23. 0.61   24. 1.70   25. 1.04   26. 0.45   27. 0.78   28. 2.04

29. 0.23   30. 2.84   31. 0.62   32. 3.62   33. 2.30   34. 0.35   35. 3.43

36. 0.86   37. 1.2   38. 1.04   39. 0.67   40. 1.62   41. 0.97   42. 1.23

Page 40:   Long Division: Remainders

1. 4,493 R5   2. 4,823 R6   3. 2,637 R5   4. 7,280 R1

5. 2,808 R1   6. 3,381 R11   7. 5,252 R2   8. 6,559 R3

9. 2,521 R4   10. 8,885 R2   11. 3,916 R10   12. 4,641 R14

13. 1,787 R5   14. 4,271 R6   15. 4,057 R0   16. 13,625 R3

17. 1,873 R9   18. 3,850 R11   19. 3,767 R7   20. 4,417 R7

21. 1,823 R8   22. 4,120 R0   23. 9,357 R7   24. 6,446 R9

25. 3,000 R0   26. 3,396 R1   27. 4,219 R2   28. 1,655 R8

Page 47:   Using the Power of 10

1. 10,000   2. 3,000,000   3. 3,000,000   4. 50,000

5. 5   6. 10,000   7. 70   8. 400,000

9. 40,000   10. 300   11. 200,000   12. 70,000

13. 100,000   14. 700   15. 300   16. 60,000

17. 500   18. 8   19. 200   20. 70

21. 800,000   22. 2   23. 60   24. 90,000

25. 90   26. 3,000,000   27. 1   28. 6

29. 900   30. 4   31. 30   32. 100

33. 70,000	34. 8,000,000	35. 8	36. 300
37. 3,000,000	38. 2,000,000	39. 7,000,000	40. 4
41. 500,000	42. 20	43. 20,000	44. 6,000,000
45. 50	46. 900,000	47. 7,000,000	48. 90,000
49. 20	50. 10,000	51. 80	52. 600
53. 100,000	54. 2	55. 30,000	56. 900
57. 60	58. 4,000,000	59. 5,000,000	60. 300

Page 52: Multiplication Word Problems

1. 24	2. 33	3. 84	4. 10	5. 98	6. 112	7. 150
8. 304	9. 120	10. 56	11. 204	12. 112	13. 180	14. 76
15. 133	16. 33	17. 144	18. 90	19. 234	20. 144	21. 180
22. 57	23. 22	24. 48	25. 150	26. 360	27. 306	28. 168
29. 342	30. 224					

Page 60: Division Word Problems

1. 59	2. 24	3. 75	4. 100	5. 67	6. 28	7. 82	8. 89
9. 86	10. 7	11. 25	12. 36	13. 27	14. 85	15. 70	16. 25
17. 16	18. 9	19. 72	20. 49	21. 56	22. 18	23. 16	24. 46
25. 5	26. 47	27. 86	28. 9	29. 48	30. 34		

Page 70: Factors

1. 2, 3, 4, 6

2. 2, 3, 4, 6, 7, 12, 14, 21, 28, 42

3. 3, 13

4. 2, 5, 7, 10, 14, 35

5. 2, 4

6. 3, 19

7. None

8. None

9. None

10. 2

11. None

12. 2, 4, 7, 14

13. None

14. 2, 4, 8, 11, 22, 44

15. 2, 3

16. None

17. 2, 3, 6, 9, 18, 27

18. None

19. None

20. 3, 9, 11, 33

21. 2, 4, 8, 16

22. 2, 4, 7, 8, 14, 28

23. None

24. 5, 19

25. 3

26. 2, 4, 8, 16, 32

27. 2, 4, 5, 10

28. None

29. 2, 23

30. 2, 4, 5, 8, 10, 20

31. None

32. 2, 41

33. None

34. 2, 4, 8

35. 7

Page 75: Multiples

1. 11, 22, 33, 44, 55

2. 78, 156, 234, 312, 390

3. 3, 6, 9, 12, 15

4. 84, 168, 252, 336, 420

5. 8, 16, 24, 32, 40

6. 45, 90, 135, 180, 225

7. 73, 146, 219, 292, 365

8. 1, 2, 3, 4, 5

9. 42, 84, 126, 168, 210

10. 7, 14, 21, 28, 35

11. 76, 152, 228, 304, 380

12. 23, 46, 69, 92, 115

13. 93, 186, 279, 372, 465

14. 69, 138, 207, 276, 345

15. 6, 12, 18, 24, 30

16. 85, 170, 255, 340, 425

17. 40, 80, 120, 160, 200

18. 54, 108, 162, 216, 270

19. 79, 158, 237, 316, 395

20. 18, 36, 54, 72, 90

21. 57, 114, 171, 228, 285

22. 34, 68, 102, 136, 170

23. 92, 184, 276, 368, 460

24. 83, 166, 249, 332, 415

25. 55, 110, 165, 220, 275

26. 4, 8, 12, 16, 20

27. 72, 144, 216, 288, 360

28. 9, 18, 27, 36, 45

29. 2, 4, 6, 8, 10

30. 68, 136, 204, 272, 340

31. 28, 56, 84, 112, 140

32. 62, 124, 186, 248, 310

33. 21, 42, 63, 84, 105

34. 41, 82, 123, 164, 205

35. 33, 66, 99, 132, 165

Page 80: Place Value

1. 7 hundreds

2. 9 tenths

3. 8 ten thousands

4. 4 tenths

5. 5 hundredths

6. 6 thousands

7. 2 hundredths

8. 2 hundreds

9. 1 hundred

10. 4 thousands

11. 2 ten thousands

12. 8 thousands

13. 5 hundreds

14. 6 ones

15. 3 thousandths

16. 4 thousands

17. 0 tenths

18. 2 millions

19. 3 ten thousands

20. 3 millions

21. 5 thousandths

22. 2 tens

23. 8 hundreds

24. 5 thousandths

25. 5 thousands

26. 3 hundreds

27. 0 hundreds

28. 9 ones

29. 0 tens

30. 2 millions

31. 5 tens

32. 8 ten thousands

33. 7 tenths

34. 1 hundred thousand

35. 8 ones

36. 2 tens

37. 2 hundreds

38. 1 ten thousand

39. 4 thousands

Page 85: Place Value: Expanded Notation

1. 37,311.07
2. 552,713.5
3. 5,960.538
4. 63,731.51
5. 817,398.5
6. 453,638.6
7. 4,536,943
8. 9,017.425
9. 3,348,999
10. 57,425.43
11. 930,484.7
12. 6,775,711
13. 2,877,624
14. 3,140,036
15. 71,760.22
16. 275,130.6
17. 367,813.5
18. 815,110.9
19. 9,605.395
20. 2,501,352
21. 1,032,247
22. 55,749.48
23. 2,571,244
24. 79,916.04

25. 693,434.9	26. 2,917.248	27. 873,496.7	28. 458,372.6
29. 6,043,358	30. 39,455.23	31. 926,764.8	32. 97,634.61
33. 18,130.08	34. 289,475.6	35. 69,831.19	36. 1,204.782
37. 9,262.402	38. 7,523,935	39. 9,033,812	40. 1,221.736

Page 91: Place Value: Expanded Notation

1. 2,514.153	2. 776,529.0	3. 23,662.91	4. 5,835.782
5. 88,700.21	6. 5,241.935	7. 62,133.42	8. 4,047.422
9. 590,761.0	10. 3,418,783	11. 42,147.96	12. 54,282.73
13. 3,252,340	14. 2,066,444	15. 2,598.860	16. 815,615.8
17. 3,955.891	18. 796,893.3	19. 94,388.01	20. 625,673.8
21. 58,014.18	22. 99,532.16	23. 397,406.8	24. 9,403,475
25. 64,748.93	26. 954,138.5	27. 5,962.703	28. 99,828.67
29. 61,569.15	30. 69,712.41	31. 3,488,903	32. 6,154,199
33. 9,117.296	34. 938,365.9	35. 9,987.198	36. 3,266,956
37. 42,086.57	38. 673,546.1	39. 9,121,582	40. 269,241.4

Page 99: Place Value: Expanded Notation

1. 6 ten thousands + 7 thousands + 3 tens + 9 ones + 4 hundredths

2. 5 millions + 6 hundred thousands + 8 ten thousands + 7 thousands + 5 hundreds + 4 tens + 6 ones

3. 8 thousands + 6 hundreds + 7 tens + 6 ones + 1 tenth + 1 hundredth + 6 thousandths

4. 3 ten thousands + 6 thousands + 2 hundreds + 4 tens + 5 ones + 7 tenths + 5 hundredths

5. 9 thousands + 7 hundreds + 3 tens + 7 tenths + 2 hundredths + 6 thousandths

6. 4 hundred thousands + 8 ten thousands + 3 thousands + 9 hundreds + 3 tens + 7 ones + 6 tenths

7. 7 millions + 5 hundred thousands + 1 ten thousand + 1 thousand + 1 hundred + 2 tens + 1 one

8. 9 millions + 7 hundred thousands + 4 ten thousands + 6 thousands + 5 hundreds + 6 tens + 3 ones

9. 1 million + 2 hundred thousands + 9 ten thousands + 5 thousands + 8 hundreds + 9 tens + 6 ones

10. 8 thousands + 8 hundreds + 2 tens + 6 ones + 9 tenths + 6 hundredths + 1 thousandth

11. 7 ten thousands + 2 thousands + 4 hundreds + 8 tens + 8 ones + 9 tenths

12. 2 millions + 2 hundred thousands + 9 ten thousands + 3 thousands + 4 hundreds + 6 tens + 9 ones

13. 8 millions + 8 ten thousands + 5 thousands + 1 hundred + 3 tens + 3 ones

14. 3 hundred thousands + 7 ten thousands + 7 thousands + 7 hundreds + 7 ones + 4 tenths

15. 5 ten thousands + 4 thousands + 2 hundreds + 3 ones + 1 tenth + 7 hundredths

16. 2 ten thousands + 5 thousands + 6 hundreds + 9 ones + 3 tenths + 6 hundredths

17. 4 ten thousands + 7 thousands + 9 hundreds + 1 ten + 2 ones + 2 tenths + 2 hundredths

18. 2 millions + 9 hundred thousands + 6 ten thousands + 2 thousands + 8 hundreds + 1 ten + 5 ones

19. 9 millions + 3 hundred thousands + 6 ten thousands + 8 hundreds + 8 tens + 8 ones

20. 9 hundred thousands + 3 ten thousands + 2 thousands + 8 hundreds + 6 tens + 3 ones + 5 tenths

21. 9 thousands + 2 hundreds + 7 tens + 9 ones + 2 tenths + 3 hundredths + 1 thousandth

22. 6 millions + 2 hundred thousands + 3 ten thousands + 4 hundreds + 7 tens + 4 ones

23. 7 millions + 8 hundred thousands + 9 ten thousands + 5 hundreds + 5 ones

24. 8 millions + 9 hundred thousands + 3 ten thousands + 6 thousands + 3 hundreds + 6 tens + 8 ones

25. 9 ten thousands + 9 thousands + 2 hundreds + 9 tens + 8 ones + 7 tenths + 9 hundredths

26. 8 ten thousands + 6 hundreds + 5 ones + 9 tenths + 5 hundredths

27. 6 millions + 3 hundred thousands + 1 ten thousand + 9 hundreds + 7 tens + 6 ones

28. 3 thousands + 8 hundreds + 6 tens + 8 ones + 6 tenths + 8 hundredths

29. 2 ten thousands + 7 hundreds + 9 tens + 2 ones + 4 tenths + 5 hundredths

30. 9 ten thousands + 3 thousands + 3 hundreds + 1 ten + 9 ones + 3 hundredths

31. 4 millions + 9 hundred thousands + 4 ten thousands + 7 thousands + 5 hundreds + 1 one

32. 7 ten thousands + 2 thousands + 2 hundreds + 4 ones + 2 tenths + 9 hundredths

33. 8 hundred thousands + 8 ten thousands + 4 thousands + 7 hundreds + 3 tens + 5 ones

34. 7 millions + 7 hundred thousands + 4 ten thousands + 6 thousands + 3 hundreds + 8 tens + 6 ones

35. 9 thousands + 5 hundreds + 5 tens + 2 ones + 8 tenths + 3 hundredths + 2 thousandths

36. 1 million + 1 hundred thousand + 1 ten thousand + 3 thousands + 8 hundreds + 7 tens + 2 ones

37. 2 thousands + 2 hundreds + 7 tens + 7 ones + 1 tenth

38. 1 hundred thousand + 3 ten thousands + 4 thousands + 9 hundreds + 4 tens + 9 ones + 3 tenths

39. 9 ten thousands + 6 thousands + 7 hundreds + 2 tens + 7 ones + 4 tenths + 8 hundredths

40. 2 millions + 6 hundred thousands + 3 ten thousands + 5 thousands + 5 hundreds + 1 ten + 8 ones

41. 3 hundred thousands + 3 thousands + 2 tens + 6 ones + 4 tenths

Page 106: Equivalent Fractions

1. 3	2. 36	3. 2	4. 10	5. 2	6. 1	7. 2	8. 15
9. 5	10. 36	11. 9	12. 9	13. 30	14. 8	15. 5	16. 20

17. 40	18. 5	19. 3	20. 20	21. 42	22. 20	23. 24	24. 35

25. 3	26. 1	27. 28	28. 9	29. 7	30. 50

Page 109: Fractions Addition (Common Denominator)

1. 10/17	2. 4/5	3. 8/13	4. 1/2	5. 10/11	6. 1/2

7. 6/7	8. 10/19	9. 3/10	10. 5/12	11. 11/13	12. 1/2

13. 5/16	14. 3/5	15. 10/11	16. 1/1	17. 5/8	18. 2/3

19. 4/5	20. 9/14	21. 3/4	22. 1/9	23. 8/9	24. 2/3

25. 5/8	26. 1/6	27. 4/5	28. 11/14	29. 9/10	30. 15/16

31. 7/9	32. 11/13	33. 2/11	34. 8/19	35. 3/5	36. 7/17

37. 5/7	38. 4/5	39. 2/3	40. 5/6	41. 14/19	42. 11/12

43. 15/16	44. 1/3	45. 1/4	46. 11/13	47. 8/9	48. 5/7

49. 7/17	50. 4/15	51. 11/20	52. 7/9	53. 5/11	54. 7/10

55. 4/5	56. 1/2	57. 11/14	58. 5/9	59. 17/20	60. 11/13

61. 1/2	62. 1/3	63. 3/5	64. 5/8	65. 10/19	66. 3/5

67. 7/10	68. 9/17	69. 4/7	70. 11/17	71. 17/20	72. 6/7

73. 1/2	74. 3/4	75. 5/6	76. 3/5	77. 8/19	78. 7/9

79. 1/2	80. 2/3	81. 9/11	82. 1/2

Page 115: Fractions Subtraction: (Common Denominator)

1. 3/16	2. 3/17	3. 1/14	4. 1/4	5. 2/5	6. 1/3

7. 1/5	8. 1/5	9. 2/17	10. 1/9	11. 1/12	12. 2/3

13. 11/17	14. 3/16	15. 1/13	16. 1/9	17. 2/5	18. 7/15

19. 6/11   20. 1/8   21. 10/19   22. 1/5   23. 7/18   24. 1/7
25. 1/7   26. 1/20   27. 1/2   28. 1/8   29. 4/7   30. 1/17
31. 1/18   32. 1/3   33. 4/19   34. 3/7   35. 1/3   36. 7/9
37. 5/11   38. 1/20   39. 1/5   40. 1/2   41. 1/15   42. 3/10
43. 6/13   44. 1/8   45. 3/8   46. 2/5   47. 1/4   48. 5/9
49. 1/11   50. 11/16   51. 9/10   52. 4/9   53. 1/10   54. 1/6
55. 1/7   56. 6/7   57. 3/19   58. 1/6   59. 2/15   60. 2/17
61. 8/19   62. 1/16   63. 5/13   64. 3/7   65. 7/11   66. 1/4
67. 1/2   68. 1/20   69. 1/5   70. 1/6   71. 12/17   72. 2/9
73. 1/10   74. 3/8   75. 1/2   76. 6/11   77. 1/13   78. 2/19
79. 7/17   80. 17/20   81. 9/16   82. 1/7

Page 121: Fractions Multiplication

1. 16/25   2. 5/18   3. 1/8   4. 1/9   5. 4/9   6. 3/32
7. 1/36   8. 2/5   9. 1/3   10. 1/64   11. 2/9   12. 9/25
13. 3/8   14. 8/25   15. 1/12   16. 25/36   17. 3/64   18. 3/25
19. 21/100   20. 1/9   21. 11/36   22. 3/8   23. 1/4   24. 3/16
25. 1/5   26. 5/18   27. 12/25   28. 21/32   29. 7/20   30. 2/9
31. 14/25   32. 12/25   33. 1/9   34. 5/36   35. 1/4   36. 1/4
37. 21/50   38. 3/16   39. 6/25   40. 1/6

Page 124: Fractions Division

1. 5/1   2. 3/2   3. 1/3   4. 1/4   5. 1/2   6. 5/4   7. 1/1

8. 2/1   9. 1/1   10. 2/1   11. 7/9   12. 1/3   13. 2/3   14. 2/1

15. 1/1   16. 1/2   17. 3/8   18. 4/5   19. 2/3   20. 3/4   21. 5/2

22. 7/9   23. 11/6   24. 7/1   25. 3/1   26. 1/1   27. 1/3   28. 2/3

29. 1/2   30. 3/2

Page 127: Area and Perimeter: Rectangles and Triangles

1. P=26 A=42

2. P=22 A=22.26

3. P=24 A=24

4. P=59 A=144

5. P=20 A=18

6. P=24 A=27.71

7. P=24 A=27.71

8. P=42 A=82.5

9. P=24 A=27.71

10. P=50 A=154

11. P=19 A=16.35

12. P=20 A=18.96

13. P=21 A=21.22

14. P=28 A=31.5

15. P=38 A=88

16. P=18 A=15.6

17. P=42 A=84.87

18. P=45 A=88.50

19. P=36 A=62.35

20. P=39 A=70.78

21. P=54 A=126

22. P=35 A=49.5

23. P=42 A=82.5

24. P=19 A=16.35

25. P=43 A=77

26. P=34 A=50

27. P=50 A=105

28. P=44 A=82.5

29. P=41 A=70

30. P=30 A=40

31. P=36 A=54

32. P=44 A=84

33. P=23 A=25.16

34. P=72 A=323

35. P=21 A=21.22

36. P=24 A=35

37. P=26 A=28

38. P=20 A=18.96

39. P=41 A=70

40. P=27 A=32

41. P=46 A=132

42. P=31 A=40.5

43. P=62 A=234

44. P=56 A=196

45. P=44 A=120

46. P=30 A=43.3

47. P=27 A=35.07

48. P=64 A=256

49. P=27 A=35.07   50. P=60 A=224   51. P=34 A=50

52. P=37 A=60

Page 140: Roman Numerals

1. 190	2. 4	3. 282	4. III
5. 185	6. 7	7. 72	8. XXXII
9. XC	10. 65	11. 95	12. 74
13. 39	14. 484	15. 1	16. LX
17. 458	18. 57	19. 56	20. LIII
21. 46	22. 8	23. XI	24. 25
25. CXXXV	26. 309	27. CDXLII	28. 85
29. CCCLVI	30. 38	31. CIX	32. CVIII
33. 83	34. II	35. LXXXIV	36. 67
37. 15	38. 37	39. LIV	40. CD
41. 368	42. 87	43. CDXI	44. 340
45. 359	46. CCLXXXVI	47. XXXVI	48. 436
49. 92	50. 22	51. CCCXV	52. 20
53. 394	54. 355	55. 101	56. XXIII
57. 35	58. 107	59. 310	60. CCLXV
61. LXXXIX	62. CDXXI	63. 16	64. 415
65. 9	66. XXVI	67. 266	68. XCIV
69. LXXIII	70. 302	71. 24	72. 110

73. 6   74. CDLVII   75. 175   76. V

77. CLVI   78. CCCXXXIII

Page 145:   Metric Weights and Measures

1. 88,000,000   2. 0.069   3. 0.00072   4. 0.000073

5. 78,000   6. 0.000022   7. 0.026   8. 0.021

9. 0.000036   10. 30,000   11. 0.047   12. 90,000

13. 0.072   14. 0.088   15. 69,000,000   16. 0.011

17. 0.85   18. 0.052   19. 0.025   20. 92,000

21. 2,600   22. 0.000028   23. 2,300,000   24. 0.000037

25. 0.000070   26. 55,000   27. 63,000   28. 0.00085

29. 0.00062   30. 0.000024   31. 74,000,000   32. 9,200,000

33. 17,000   34. 0.080   35. 34,000   36. 0.052

37. 0.00039   38. 21,000   39. 0.050   40. 0.027

Page 148:   Metric Conversion

1. 0.660   2. 0.787   3. 18.288   4. 1.753   5. 2.464

6. 24.384   7. 4.572   8. 8.534   9. 24.689   10. 15.240

11. 3.658   12. 2.108   13. 0.254   14. 1.930   15. 1.067

16. 1.778   17. 17.069   18. 13.716   19. 3.962   20. 0.838

21. 1.473   22. 0.991   23. 1.473   24. 0.584   25. 17.069

26. 16.459   27. 25.298   28. 2.311   29. 1.626   30. 8.230

31. 1.803   32. 22.555   33. 3.658   34. 2.464   35. 23.165

36. 2.413   37. 20.422   38. 1.346   39. 12.192   40. 27.127